# Lion Brand Yarn

# Vintage Styles for Today

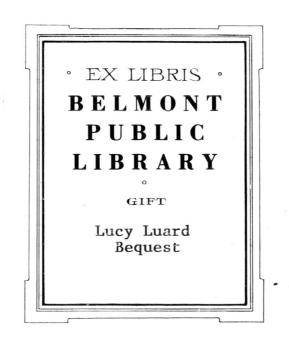

# Lion Brand Yarn

# Vintage Styles for Today

MORE THAN 50 PATTERNS
TO KNIT AND CROCHET

edited by Nancy J. Thomas
and Charlotte J. Quiggle

POTTER
CRAFT

NEW YORK

Copyright ©2006 by Lion Brand Yarn Company

All rights reserved.

Published in the United States by Potter Craft,

an imprint of the Crown Publishing Group,

a division of Random House, Inc., New York.

www.crownpublishing.com

www.clarksonpotter.com

POTTER CRAFT and CLARKSON N. POTTER are trademarks and Potter and colophon are

registered trademarks of Random House, Inc.

Library of Congress Cataloging-in-Publication Data is available.

ISBN 1-4000-8061-4

Printed in Singapore

Design by Element group

Vintage archival photographs courtesy of Lion Brand Yarn Company

All other photography by Jack Deutsch

10   9   8   7   6   5   4   3   2   1

First Edition

# Acknowledgments

*Lion Brand Yarn: Vintage Styles for Today* would not have been possible without the hard work and dedication of many people.

Design editor Susan Haviland took on the (until now) thankless task of coordinating all the patterns, yarn, and sample knitters and crocheters while at the same time checking patterns and producing several of the samples. We are equally grateful to Associate Design Editor Stephanie Klose. Doris Chan, Marianne Forrestal, and Heather Lodinsky recreated patterns and provided beautiful knitting and crocheting. Bobbi Anderson, Jeannie Chin, Mary DuBois, Cindy Grosch, Sara Harper, Jodi Lewanda, Margarita Mejia, Shirley Okerstrom, Charlotte Quiggle, and Judy Sumner toiled with hooks and needles, creating samples far into the night with lovely results. Technical editor Karen Frisa loaned her meticulous eye and extensive knowledge. Many thanks to stylist Drew Biase and photographer Jack Deutsch for creating the beautiful photographs in the book. Thanks also to Fashion Editor Rebecca Rosen for orchestrating the photography and styling. We are also indebted to Rose Mary Perez, Daniel Soltis, and Janet Vetter for their assistance with schematics and charts; to Glee Barre, who drew the technical illustrations; and to Ann Kirby Payne for her superb editing skills.

The Craft Yarn Council of America generously provided the Yarn Weight Standards and accompanying icons used in this book. (For more information, please visit www.yarnstandards.com.)

Finally, we are grateful to the legendary Blumenthal family and the Lion Brand Yarn Company, who made the archived material available for the book. We especially honor Isidor Blumenthal, who dedicated his long and successful professional life to the service of knitters and crocheters, both past and present. Special thanks to David Blumenthal and Dean Blumenthal, who will take us into the future.

# Contents

# Introduction

At Lion Brand Yarns, we've spent more than a century shaping the future of knitting and crochet, while preserving the past. With this book, we are showcasing the unbroken thread linking our nineteenth- and twentieth-century yarns and patterns to the knitter and crocheter of the twenty-first century.

In 1916, Lion Brand published a pattern book that "embodied a carefully selected line from both home and abroad of the newest creations in Worsted work, together with a few of the old styles which retain their popularity." Even then, knitters recognized the value of older "vintage" patterns! Since everything old is new again, we are including many of those same patterns in this book (as well as patterns for garments from the decades in-between) reinterpreted in today's yarns.

The styles we've selected may come from different eras, but they all share a timeless quality. Most of the pieces are simple enough for a beginner to tackle yet provide enough interest to hold the attention of more experienced needleworkers. We've updated the instructions to make the language and format more familiar to today's knitters and crocheters and have made a few adjustments to the way the garments fit. We've also increased the number of sizes offered to include a wider range for today's bodies. The result is a timeless collection of patterns for garments for the entire family (including the dog!) and accessories for the home. We hope that you'll feel a connection to the past while you knit or crochet these pieces, any of which may become tomorrow's heirloom.

# A Few Notes about Vintage Patterns

All of the styles shown in this book are adapted from original patterns in the Lion Brand archives. Finding your own vintage knitting and crochet patterns can be a fairly simple undertaking. Flea markets, thrift stores, antique shops, and tag sales are all gold mines for vintage pattern booklets, needlework magazines, and leaflets; they're also excellent places to find old copies of women's magazines, most of which usually include a pattern or two for a knit or crocheted garment or afghan. An Internet search under "vintage knitting patterns" or "knitting history" will turn up dozens of sites that offer copies of patterns from the past hundred years or so; similarly, auction sites such as eBay are rich with vintage offerings. In addition, you will find that textile museums and many libraries can be treasure troves of both old pattern books and samples of knitwear from days gone by.

# Making It Your Own

Once you've found a vintage garment you like, you'll need to evaluate not only how wearable it is but also how easily the pattern can be adapted to suit your size, knitting skill, and lifestyle. Hats, mittens, blankets, and afghans rarely need more than a re-gauging to accommodate your choice of current yarn to make them "modern"; the same goes for classic cardigans, shawls, and pullovers. Some styles, however, may require a bit more fine-tuning to reflect today's more relaxed fit. For example, the fitted shapes of the 1940s, 1950s, and early 1960s involved a higher, closer-fitting armhole, a more nipped-in waist, and less "wiggle room" than we are accustomed to today.

You will also find that yesterday's sizes are drastically different from those of today. Once upon a time, clothing manufacturers (and knitwear pattern writers) conformed to a standardized chart of measurements. Today, however, you can try on several pairs of pants and discover that the size that fits your body can vary by as much as three sizes; even within the same brand there is little consistency. In addition, the pre-World War I sizing charts assumed that all women wore corsets (which crushed the waist while lowering the bosom), while those of the 1930s and 1950s factored in sturdy girdles and structured bras. Although corsets disappeared during the flapper days of the 1920s, and ladies had to lose their girdles during World War II (when rubber was rationed), the average woman was thinner during those years than she is today. Therefore, since our bodies are so different today from those of our forebears, whether because of undergarments or because of diet, any reference to "size" in a vintage pattern is relatively meaningless.

# Making Sense of Instructions

Knitters and crocheters accustomed to today's detailed pattern instructions may find themselves a bit lost when trying to decipher instructions for vintage styles. The pattern writers of old assumed a certain amount of knowledge on the part of the needleworker attempting the project and often left out finishing instructions as well as other key information such as gauge and finished measurements. Rather than tell the knitter which decrease to use in what situation, they would just write "n," which stood for "narrow." In addition, their patterns were very word-dense because they wrote out all stitch instructions (including those for cables and colorwork) rather than provide a chart as a visual guide as is generally done today.

The instructions for the projects in this book have all been reworked to make them more familiar to the modern needleworker; should you decide to undertake working up your own favorite vintage pattern, read through all of the instructions before you begin so that you understand what is required to complete the piece.

# Substituting Yarns

Finding the exact yarn used for the garment in the original vintage pattern is an unlikely prospect. So how do you go about making a substitution? Start with the fabric. If, for example, you want to keep to the original look and fit of a garment that was worked at a fine gauge (say, 7 or 8 stitches to the inch), start with a plain sportweight yarn and knit or crochet a swatch to find a fabric that you like. Always work a gauge swatch *at least 4 inches (10 cm) square*. Do not measure it until you have removed it from the needles (preferably bound off), washed it in the manner in which the finished garment will be washed, and blocked it. Experiment with different needle sizes and yarns until you are satisfied. If you are working on a post-World War II pattern, you are more likely to be given a gauge for which to aim.

When knitting any of the patterns in this book, use the yarn called for in the materials section to make an exact duplicate of the project shown in the accompanying photograph. If you'd rather substitute your own yarn, choose one in the same weight category with comparable fiber content as the yarn used in the instructions. You'll find this information printed on the yarn label and in the pattern instructions. The Standard Yarn Weight System chart on page 13 will help you compare the two. Create a swatch to make certain your substitution matches the gauge called for in the pattern. To determine how much of the substitute yarn you will need, multiply the number of balls called for in the pattern by the yards/meters per ball. Divide this figure by the yards/meters per ball listed on the label of the substitute yarn. Round up to the next whole number; this is how many balls you will need to purchase.

# Abbreviations

beg = begin(ning)

CC = contrasting color

ch = chain

ch-space = space previously made

cont = continu(e)(ing)

dc = double crochet

dc2tog = double crochet 2 together

dec = decreas(e)(s)(ing)

dpn = double-pointed needles

dtr = double treble (triple) crochet

hdc = half double crochet

inc = increas(e)(s)(ing)

k = knit

k2tog = knit 2 together

k3tog = knit 3 together

MC = main color

p = purl

p2tog = purl 2 together

psso = pass slipped stitch over

Rev St st = reverse stockinette stitch

rnd(s) = round(s)

RS = right side

sc = single crochet

sc2tog = single crochet 2 together

sc3tog = single crochet 3 together

St st = stockinette stitch

st(s) = stitch(es)

t-ch = turning chain

tog = together

tr = treble (triple) crochet

WS = wrong side

yo = yarn over

# Standards for Crochet and Knitting

## SIZE AND FIT FOR WOMEN

**Very-close fitting:** Actual chest/bust measurement or less

**Close-fitting:** 1–2"/2.5–5cm

**Standard-fitting:** 2–4"/5–10cm

**Loose-fitting:** 4–6"/10–15cm

**Oversized:** 6"/15cm or more

## LENGTH FOR WOMEN

**Waist length:** Actual body measurement

**Hip length:** 6"/15cm down from waist

**Tunic length:** 11"/28cm down from waist

| Woman's size | X-Small | Small | Medium | Large | 1X | 2X |
|---|---|---|---|---|---|---|
| **1.** Bust (in.) | 28–30 | 32–34 | 36–38 | 40–42 | 44–46 | 48–50 |
| *(cm.)* | *71–76* | *81–86* | *91.5–96.5* | *101.5–106.5* | *111.5–117* | *122–127* |
| **2.** Center Back Neck-to-Cuff | 27–27½ | 28–28½ | 29–29½ | 30–30½ | 31–31½ | 31½–32 |
| | *68.5–70* | *71–72.5* | *73.5–75* | *76–77.5* | *78.5–80* | *80–81.5* |
| **3.** Back Waist Length | 16½ | 17 | 17¼ | 17½ | 17¾ | 18 |
| | *42* | *43* | *43.5* | *44.5* | *45* | *45.5* |
| **4.** Cross Back (Shoulder to Shoulder) | 14–14½ | 14½–15 | 16–16½ | 17–17½ | 17½ | 18 |
| | *35.5–37* | *37–38* | *40.5–42* | *43–44.5* | *44.5* | *45.5* |
| **5.** Sleeve Length to Underarm | 16½ | 17 | 17 | 17½ | 17½ | 18 |
| | *42* | *43* | *43* | *44.5* | *44.5* | *45.5* |

| Man's size | Small | Medium | Large | 1X | 2X |
|---|---|---|---|---|---|
| **1.** Chest (in.) | 34-36 | 38-40 | 42-44 | 46-48 | 50-52 |
| *(cm.)* | *86-91.5* | *96.5-101.5* | *106.5-111.5* | *116.5-111* | *127-132* |
| **2.** Center Back Neck-to-Cuff | 32-32½ | 33-33½ | 34-34½ | 35-35½ | 36-36½ |
| | *81-82.5* | *83.5-85* | *86.5-87.5* | *89-90* | *91.5-92.5* |
| **3.** Back Hip Length | 25-25½ | 26½-26¾ | 27-27½ | 27½-27¾ | 28-2½ |
| | *63.5-64.5* | *67.5-68* | *68.5-69* | *69.5-70.5* | *71-72.5* |
| **4.** Cross Back (Shoulder to Shoulder) | 15½-16 | 16½-17 | 17½-18 | 18-18½ | 18½-19 |
| | *39.5-40.5* | *42-43* | *44.5-45.5* | *45.5-47* | *47-48* |
| **5.** Sleeve Length to Underarm | 18 | 18½ | 19½ | 20 | 20½ |
| | *45.5* | *47* | *49.5* | *50.5* | *52* |

## HEAD CIRCUMFERENCE CHART

| | Infant/Child | | | | Adult | |
|---|---|---|---|---|---|---|
| | Preemie | Baby | Toddler | Child | Woman | Man |
| **1.** Circumference (in.) | 12 | 14 | 16 | 18 | 20 | 22 |
| *(cm.)* | *30.5* | *35.5* | *40.5* | *45.5* | *50.5* | *56* |

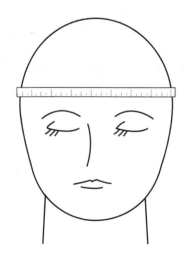

For an accurate head measurement, place a tape measure across the forehead and measure around the full circumference of the head. Keep the tape snug for accurate results.

## Categories of yarn, gauge ranges, and recommended needle and hook sizes

| Yarn Weight Symbol & Category Names | 1 Super Fine | 2 Fine | 3 Light | 4 Medium | 5 Bulky | 6 Super Bulky |
|---|---|---|---|---|---|---|
| Types of Yarns in Category | Sock, Fingering, Baby | Sport, Baby | DK, Light Worsted | Worsted, Afghan Aran | Chunky, Craft, Rug | Bulky, Roving |
| Knit Gauge Range* in Stockinette Stitch to 4 inches | 27–32 sts | 23–26 sts | 21–24 sts | 16–20 sts | 12–15 sts | 6–11 sts |
| Recommended Needle in Metric Size Range | 2.25–3.25 mm | 3.25–3.75 mm | 3.75–4.5 mm | 4.5–5.5 mm | 5.5–8 mm | 8 mm and larger |
| Recommended Needle U.S. Size Range | 1 to 3 | 3 to 5 | 5 to 7 | 7 to 9 | 9 to 11 | 11 and larger |
| Crochet Gauge* Ranges in Single Crochet to 4 inch | 21–32 sts | 16–20 sts | 12–17 sts | 11–14 sts | 8–11 sts | 5–9 sts |
| Recommended Hook in Metric Size Range | 2.25–3.5 mm | 3.5–4.5 mm | 4.5–5.5 mm | 5.5–6.4 mm | 6.5–9 mm | 9 mm and larger |
| Recommended Hook U.S. Size Range | B-1 to E-4 | E-4 to 7 | 7 to I-9 | I-9 to K-10½ | K-10½ to M-13 | M-13 and larger |

*GUIDELINES ONLY: The above reflect the most commonly used gauges and needle or hook sizes for specific yarn categories.

# CHAPTER 1

# Always the Lady: Cardigans and Jackets

Cardigans and knit jackets were (and still are) the staple of every woman's wardrobe. Combining comfort with classic chic, they offer an instant, effortless way to pull together an outfit and complement everything from dinner dresses to jeans and tees.

The designs on the following pages not only transcend the seasons (with a change of color or fiber they'll work from the first hint of cold, straight through until spring), they also sail through time, looking as great today as they did when they first debuted.

# The Everyday Jacket

Doubtless designed as a cozy cover-up to chase off the early hour chill as one walked the garden, this strikingly simple piece didn't need much updating. Fast, easy, and fun to knit, it's perfect for an early morning latte fix or a lazy autumn afternoon of antiquing.

KNIT **EASY +**

## SIZES

S (M, L, 1X, 2X, 3X)

**Finished chest, buttoned** 39 (43, 47, 51, 55, 59)" [99 (109, 119.5, 129.5, 139.5, 150) cm]

**Length** 25 (25 1/2, 26, 26 1/2, 27, 28) [63.5 (65, 66, 67.5, 68.5, 71) cm]

**Note** Before beginning pattern, circle all numbers pertaining to your size for ease in working.

## MATERIALS

(**5**) LION BRAND Color Waves

*3 oz (85 g) 125 yd (113 m) Skein*

*83% Acrylic 17% Polyester*

- 6 (7, 7, 8, 9, 9) skeins #398 Pebble Beach (MC)
- 2 (2, 2, 3, 3, 3) skeins #347 Purple Vista (CC)
  or colors of your choice
- Size 10.5 (6.5 mm) 29" (70 cm) circular needle OR SIZE TO OBTAIN GAUGE
- Spare circular needle to use as stitch holder
- Satin ribbon 1/2" (13 mm) wide, 42" (106.5 cm) long (optional)
- Large-eyed, blunt needle

## GAUGE

11 sts + 22 rows = 4" (10 cm) in Garter Stitch (knit every row).

BE SURE TO CHECK YOUR GAUGE.

NOTE This garment is worked in one piece starting at the bottom Back, casting on sts for the Sleeves, working over the shoulders and down the Fronts. The holes in the Collar for the ribbon tie are optional.

## JACKET

With MC, cast on 54 (59, 65, 70, 76, 81) sts using a provisional cast on (see Techniques, page 188). Work in Garter Stitch for 15 (15, 14 1/2, 14 1/2, 14, 14)" [38 (38, 37, 37, 35.5, 35.5) cm], ending with a WS row.

**Sleeves**

Cast on 38 (35, 34, 32, 31, 30) sts at end of next 2 rows for Sleeves—130 (129, 133, 134, 138, 141) sts. Work even for 9 1/2 (10, 11, 11 1/2, 12 1/2, 13 1/2)" [24 (25.5, 28, 29, 32, 34.5) cm], ending with a WS row.

**Divide for back neck**

K 56 (55, 57, 57, 58, 59) sts, join 2nd ball of yarn, bind off center 18 (19, 19, 20, 22, 23) sts for back neck, knit to end of row. Working both sides at same time, knit 6 rows.

**Shape front neck**

Inc one st at each neck edge every other row 4 times, then cast on 5 (5, 5, 6, 7, 7) sts at neck edge—65 (64, 66, 67, 69, 70) sts each side. Work even until front of Sleeve measures same as back of Sleeve. Bind off 38 (35, 34, 32, 31, 30) sts at beg of next 2 rows—27 (29, 32, 35, 38, 40) sts each side. Work even until Fronts measure same as Back, ending with a WS row. Transfer sts to spare circular needle for holder.

## Cuffs

With RS facing and CC, pick up and knit one st in each garter ridge along edge of Sleeve. Knit 18 rows. Bind off loosely. Sew side and Sleeve seams.

## Front and bottom bands

With RS facing and CC, beg at Left Front neck edge, pick up and knit one st in each garter ridge down Left Front; knit sts from holder and provisional cast on along bottom of Jacket; pick up and knit one st in each garter ridge up Right Front. Knit 1 row, marking corner sts.

**Inc Row (RS)** Knit to corner st, yarn over, k 1, yarn over, k to next corner st, yarn over, k 1, yarn over, knit to end. Repeat Inc Row every other row 7 more times. Bind off loosely.

## Collar

With RS facing and CC, pick up and knit 42 (43, 43, 46, 50, 51) sts around neck. Knit 3 rows.

**Ribbon hole row (optional)** Knit 0 (0, 0, 2, 1, 1) sts, *k 3, yarn over, k2tog; repeat from * 7 (7, 7, 7, 8, 8) more times, end k 2 (3, 3, 4, 4, 5).

**Next row** Knit all sts, including yarn overs. Bind off 4 sts at beg of next 2 rows—34 (35, 35, 38, 42, 43) sts. Knit 26 rows. Bind off loosely. Weave in ends.

**Optional** Weave ribbon through holes in Collar.

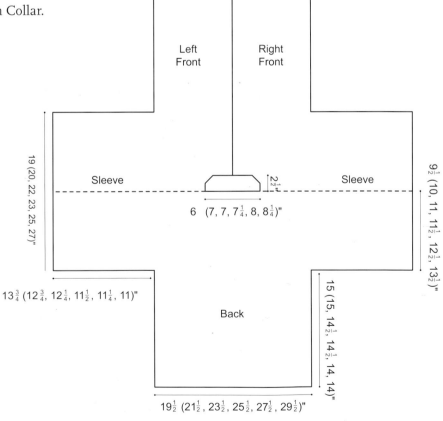

# The City Coat and Square Tam

Chic, simple, and almost as effortless to make as it is to wear, this sleek little coat just oozes style. The fold-over collar draws attention to the face, and subtle shaping makes it the perfect flatter-your-figure alternative to a bulky jacket. We upped the impact by using a silky soft, multi-tonal yarn, and chunky stitches make for fast knitting. Top it off with an oversized tam, trimmed with crocheted roses.

KNIT with CROCHET edging **EASY**

## SIZES

S (M, L, 1X, 2X)

**Finished chest, buttoned** 40 (44, 48, 52, 56, 60)" [101.5 (112, 122, 132, 142, 152.5) cm]

**Length** 26" (66 cm)

**Note** Before beginning pattern, circle all numbers pertaining to your size for ease in working.

## MATERIALS

(5) LION BRAND Homespun
*6 oz (70 g) 185 yd (169 m) Skein*
*98% Acrylic 2% Polyester*

- 7 (8, 9, 9 10, 11) skeins #362 Quartz or color of your choice
- Size 10 (6 mm) 29" (70 cm) circular knitting needle OR SIZE TO OBTAIN GAUGE
- Size K-10.5 (6.5 mm) crochet hook OR SIZE TO OBTAIN GAUGE
- Stitch markers
- Large-eyed, blunt needle
- Five 1" (25 mm) buttons

## GAUGE

14 sts + 28 rows = 4" (10 cm) in Garter Stitch (knit every row).

10 sc + 10 rows = 4" (10 cm).

BE SURE TO CHECK YOUR GAUGE.

**NOTES** This jacket is knit in one piece, starting at bottom Back and casting on for Sleeves. The piece is divided for back neck and worked over shoulders to Fronts, which are worked one at a time from shoulders down.

Collar, cuffs, and bands are crocheted separately and sewn on after the piece is knit.

## coat

### BACK

Cast on 70 (77, 84, 91, 98, 105) sts. Work in Garter Stitch until piece measures 18$^1/_2$ (19, 17$^1/_2$, 17, 16, 15$^1/_2$)" [47 (48, 44.5, 43, 40.5, 39.5) cm] or desired length to armhole, ending with a WS row.

### SLEEVES

At beginning of next two rows, cast on 52 (49, 49, 46, 46, 42) stitches using cable cast on method (see Techniques, page 188) for Sleeves—174 (175, 182, 183, 190, 189) stitches. Work even until piece measures 26" (66 cm) from beg or desired length to shoulders.

**Divide for back neck** K 78 (77, 80, 79, 82, 81) sts, join second skein of yarn and bind off center 18 (21, 22, 25, 26, 27) sts, knit to end. Working left and right sides separately, and AT THE SAME TIME, knit 7 rows, place marker for center shoulder, knit 7 rows.

## FRONTS

Inc one stitch at neck edge every other row 21 times—99 (98, 101, 100, 103, 102) stitches. Work even until Front Sleeve measures same as Back Sleeve from marker. Bind off 52 (49, 49, 46, 46, 42) Sleeve stitches—47 (49, 52, 54, 57, 60) st remain. Work even until Fronts measure same as Back. Bind off.

## FINISHING

### Collar

Chain 21. **Row 1** Sc in 2nd ch from hook and in each ch across—20 sc.

**Row 2** Ch 1, turn. Sc in each sc across. Repeat Row 2 until Collar is long enough to fit into neck opening. Fasten off. Sew Collar into neck opening.

### Left front band

**Row 1** With right side facing, work 1 row sc between top of Collar and bottom of Front.

**Row 2** Sc in each st to neck edge, ch 2, skip 2; sc to end of row.

**Row 3** Sc in all sts, including each ch of ch2. Fasten off.

### Buttonhole band (Right Front)

**Row 1** With RS facing, work 1 row sc between top of Collar and bottom of Front.

**Row 2 (buttonholes)** Mark four buttonhole positions as follows: one at neck edge, one 10" (25 cm) from bottom of garment, and two evenly spaced between the top and bottom buttons. Sc to first buttonhole marker, *ch 2, skip 2, sc to next marker; repeat from * 3 times more, sc to end of row.

**Row 3** Sc across all stitches, including each ch of ch2s. Fasten off.

### Cuffs—Make 2

Work as for Collar until piece measures 11 (11¹/₂, 12, 12¹/₂, 13, 14)" [28 (29, 30.5, 32, 33, 35.5) cm]. Fasten off. Sew Cuff onto bottom of Sleeve, easing Sleeve fabric into Cuff.

### Edging

With RS facing, work reverse sc along edges of Collar, Bands, and Cuffs.

Sew side and underarm seams. Fold back Cuff and tack in place.

### Buttons

Try on Jacket and mark positions for buttons on Left Front opposite buttonholes. Sew buttons in place.

### Interior fastenings

Mark position for button on Right Front opposite buttonhole on Left Front Band. Sew button in place.

### Ties

Make 12" (30 cm)–long chain. Fasten securely 10" (25 cm) down from neck edge on Right Front. Mark position on Left Front opposite tie. Make 12"- (30 cm-)long chain at marked position.

Schematic measurements:

13½ (14, 14¾, 15½, 16¼, 17)"

Left Front · Right Front

11 (11½, 12, 12½, 13, 14)"

Crochet Cuff · Left Sleeve · Right Sleeve

17 (16, 19, 20, 22, 23)"

8"

5 (6, 6¼, 7, 7¼, 7½)"

2"

14¾ (14, 14, 13, 13, 12)"

Back

18½ (19, 17½, 17, 16, 15½)"

20 (22, 24, 26, 28, 30)"

# square tam

### SIZE
One size fits most

### MATERIALS
(4) LION BRAND Wool-Ease

*3 oz (85 g) 197 yd (180 m) Ball*

*80% Acrylic, 20% Wool*

- 2 balls #147 Purple
  or color of your choice
- Sizes G-6 and H-8 (4 and 5 mm)
  crochet hooks OR SIZE TO OBTAIN
  GAUGE
- Large-eyed, blunt needle

### GAUGE
18 stitches = 4" (10 cm) in Flat Knot
Stitch on smaller hook.
BE SURE TO CHECK YOUR GAUGE.

### STITCH EXPLANATIONS

#### FLAT KNOT STITCH
**Row 1** Skip first chain, *single crochet in next stitch, double crochet in following stitch; repeat from * to last chain, single crochet in last chain.

**Row 2** Chain 1, *single crochet into single crochet of previous row, double crochet into double crochet of previous row; repeat from * across, end single crochet in last single crochet. Repeat Row 2 for pattern.

#### CLUSTER STITCH
**Round 1** Ch 1, sc in first sc, ch 1, draw up a loop in each of next 3 sc, yarn over and draw through all 4 loops on hook, *ch 1, draw up a loop in same stitch as last cluster loop, draw up a loop in each of next 2 sc, yarn over and draw through all 4 loops on hook; repeat from *, join with slip stitch in top of beg sc.

**Round 2** Ch 1, draw up a loop in top of first sc, [draw up a loop in ch1-space, draw up loop in next cluster, yarn over and draw through all 4 loops, *ch 1, draw up a loop in same stitch as last cluster loop, draw up a loop in ch1-space, draw up a loop in next cluster, yarn over and draw through all 4 loops; repeat from * around, join with slip stitch in top of first cluster. Ch 1.]

**Round 3** Draw up a loop in first cluster, repeat between [ ] in Round 2. Repeat Round 3 to desired size.

#### HAT
With smaller hook, ch 26. Work in Flat Knot Stitch, increasing one st at beg and end of every row until work measures 16" (41 cm) in width and 6 1/2" (16.5 cm) in length. Work even for 5" (13 cm), then decrease one st at beg and end of every row until 25 sc remain. Hat should now resemble an octagon in shape.

#### FINISHING
**Band** Work 1 sc into each of 25 sts, skip diagonal edge, then work 15 sc along straight side of work. Work 25 sc along foundation ch and 15 sc on other straight side of work and join—80 sc. Work sc all around until Band measures 2 3/4" (7 cm). Turn work WS out and work 1 row of sc through back loops only. Work 8 rows of Cluster Stitch for turn-back on band. Do not fasten off.

**Picot edge** Ch 1, *(sc, ch 3, sc) into same space, skip 1; repeat from * around. Gather diagonal edge and sew down. Trim with Flower.

## FLOWER

With larger hook and 2 strands held tog, ch 5, slip stitch in first ch to form ring.

**Round 1** Ch 3, 9 dc in ring, join with slip stitch to top of beg ch—10 sts.

**Round 2** Ch 2, working in front loops only, 2 hdc in each dc around. Join with slip stitch to top of beg ch—20 sts.

**Round 3** Ch 1, *sc, sc2tog; repeat from * around, end with sc, join with slip stitch to top of beg sc. Fasten off.

**Round 4** With RS facing, join yarn to back loop of Round 1. Ch 4, 3 tr in each back loop around, join with slip stitch to top of beg ch—30 stitches.

**Round 5** Ch 1, *sc, sc2tog; repeat from * around, end with sc, join with slip stitch to top of beg sc. Fasten off.

# The All-Seasons Cardigan

Some things are timeless in their appeal. Take this classic cardigan, for example. Perfectly placed faux cables and a flattering shawl collar look as good today as they did way back—we simply substituted a super-soft, super-light microfiber yarn for the original wool. The result is a season-spanning sweater that transitions easily from an air-conditioned office to an evening al fresco.

KNIT with CROCHET button loops **INTERMEDIATE**

## SIZES

S (M, L, 1X, 2X, 3X)

**Finished chest, buttoned** 37 (41, 45, 49, 53, 57)" [94 (104, 114.5, 124.5, 134.5, 145) cm]

**Length** 25 1/4 (25 1/4, 25 3/4, 26 1/4, 27 1/4, 27 3/4)" [64 (64, 65.5, 66.5, 69, 70.5) cm]

**Note** Before beginning pattern, circle all numbers pertaining to your size for ease in working.

## MATERIALS

**(3)** LION BRAND Microspun
*2 1/2 oz (70 g) 168 yd (154 m) Ball*
*100 % Microfiber Acrylic*

- 9 (9, 10, 11, 12, 13) balls #124 Mocha or color of your choice
- Size 5 (3.75 mm) knitting needles OR SIZE TO OBTAIN GAUGE
- Size F-5 (3.75 mm) crochet hook
- Seven 1" (25 mm) buttons
- Large-eyed, blunt needle

## GAUGE

24 sts + 32 rows = 4" (10 cm) in over Faux-Cable pattern.
24 sts + 48 rows = 4" (10 cm) in Garter Stitch (k every row).
BE SURE TO CHECK YOUR GAUGE

## NOTES

Work decreases one stitch in from edge, maintaining one stitch selvage in Stockinette stitch (k on RS, p on WS). On RS, right edge decrease is ssk (see Techniques, page 188), left edge decrease is k2tog. On WS, right edge decrease is p2tog, left edge decrease is ssp. (see Techniques, p. 188) Work Sleeve increases 2 stitches in from edge, maintaining two stitch selvage in Stockinette stitch.

## PATTERN STITCH

### FAUX-CABLE PATTERN (multiple of 6 sts)

**Row 1 (RS)** *K 1, p 1, k 1; repeat from *.
**Row 2** *P 1, k 1, yo, k 2, pass the yarn over over the k 2, k 1, p 1; repeat from *.
**Row 3** *K 1, p 4, k 1; repeat from *.
**Row 4** *K 2, p 2, k 2; repeat from *.
Repeat Rows 1–4 for Faux-Cable Pattern.

## BACK

Cast on 110 (122, 134, 146, 158, 170) sts. Work in Garter Stitch for 1 1/2" (4 cm), ending with a WS row.

**Next Row (RS)** K 1, work in Faux-Cable Pattern to last st, k 1. Work even in Faux-Cable Pattern. Cont in Pattern Stitch, maintaining first and last sts in St st, for 39 more rows.

**Dec Row (RS)** K 1, ssk, work in pattern to last 3 sts, k2tog, k 1—108 (120, 132, 144, 156, 168) sts. Repeat Dec Row every 40th row 2 more times—104 (116, 128, 140, 152, 164) sts remain. Work even until piece measures 16 1/2 (16 1/2, 16 1/2, 16 1/2, 17, 16 1/2)" [42 (42, 42, 42, 43, 42) cm] from beg, ending with a WS row.

**Shape armholes** Bind off 7 (9, 11, 12, 14, 16) sts at beg of next 2 rows. Dec one st each end every other row 7 (9, 10, 12, 13, 15) times—76 (80, 86, 92, 98, 102) sts [see Notes]. Work even in pattern until armhole measures 8 (8, 8½, 9, 9½, 10½)" [20.5 (20.5, 21.5, 23, 24, 26.5) cm] from beg of shaping, ending with a WS row.

**Shape shoulders** Bind off 6 sts at beg of next 2 (2, 0, 0, 0, 0) rows; 7 sts at beg of next 4 (4, 4, 2, 0, 0) rows; 8 sts at beg of next 0 (0, 2, 4, 4, 2) rows; and 9 sts at beg of next 0 (0, 0, 0, 2, 4) rows—36 (40, 42, 46, 48, 50) sts. Bind off.

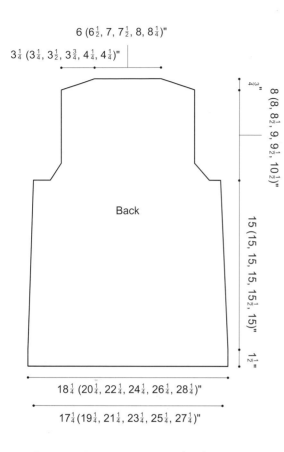

6 (6½, 7, 7½, 8, 8¼)"

3¼ (3¼, 3½, 3¾, 4¼, 4¼)"

Back

¾"

8 (8, 8½, 9, 9½, 10½)"

15 (15, 15, 15, 15½, 15)"

1½"

18¼ (20¼, 22¼, 24¼, 26¼, 28¼)"

17¼ (19¼, 21¼, 23¼, 25¼, 27¼)"

## LEFT FRONT

Cast on 57 (63, 69, 75, 81, 87) sts. Work in Garter Stitch for 1½" (4 cm), ending with a WS row. Set up pattern as follows:

**Row 1 (RS)** K 1, work in Faux-Cable Pattern to last 2 sts, k 2.
**Row 2** P 2, work in Faux-Cable Pattern to last st, p 1.
**Row 3** Repeat Row 1.
**Row 4** P 1, k 1, work in Faux-Cable Pattern to last st, p 1.
Cont in pattern as established, maintaining first and last sts in St st, for 36 more rows.

**Dec Row (RS)** K 1, ssk, work in pattern to last 2 sts, k 2—56 (62, 68, 74, 80, 86) sts. Repeat Dec Row every 40th row 2 more times–54 (60, 66, 72, 78, 84) sts. Work even until piece measures same as Back to armholes, ending with a WS row.

**Shape armhole** Bind off 7 (9, 11, 12, 14, 16) sts at beg of next row. Dec one st at armhole edge every other row 7 (9, 10, 12, 13, 15) times and, AT THE SAME TIME, when armhole measures ¾" (2 cm) from beg of shaping, begin neck shaping.

**Shape neck** Dec one st at neck edge (see Notes) every other row 3 (9, 8, 10, 9, 4) times, then every 3rd row 17 (13, 15, 15, 17, 23) times—20 (20, 22, 23, 25, 26) sts. Work until armhole measures same as Back to shoulders, ending with a WS row.

**Shape shoulder** Bind off 6 sts at beg of next 1 (1, 0, 0, 0, 0) row; 7 sts at beg of next 2 (2, 2, 1, 0, 0) RS rows; 8 sts at beg of next 0 (0, 1, 2, 2, 1) RS rows; and 9 sts at beg of next 0 (0, 0, 0, 1, 2) RS rows.

## RIGHT FRONT

Work as for Left Front, reversing shaping. Set up pattern as follows:

**Row 1 (RS)** K 2, work in Faux-Cable Pattern to last st, k 1.
**Row 2** P 1, work in Faux-Cable Pattern to last 2 sts, p 2.
**Row 3** Repeat Row 1.
**Row 4** P 1, work in Faux-Cable Pattern to last 2 sts, k 1, p 1.

## SLEEVES

Cast on 46 (52, 58, 58, 64, 70) sts. Work in Garter Stitch for 3" (7.5 cm), ending with a WS row. Set up pattern as follows:

**Row 1** (RS) K 2, work in Faux-Cable Pattern to last 2 sts, k 2.

**Row 2** P 2, work in Faux-Cable Pattern to last 2 sts, p 2. Cont in pattern as established, maintaining 2 st selvage at each edge (see Notes) and, AT THE SAME TIME, inc one st each end every 4th row 0 (5, 5, 12, 12, 23) times, then every 5th row 25 (20, 20, 16, 16, 8) times—96 (102, 108, 114, 120, 132) sts. Work even in pattern until piece measures 19 (19, 19, 19 1/2, 19 1/2, 20)" [48.5 (48.5, 48.5, 49.5, 49.5, 51) cm] from beg, ending with a WS row.

**Shape cap** Bind off 7 (9, 11, 12, 14, 16) sts at beg of next two rows. Dec one st each end every row 22 (24, 19, 18, 14, 13) times, then every other row 3 (1, 6, 8, 12, 15) times. Bind off remaining 32 (34, 36, 38, 40, 44) sts.

## BACK BELT (OPTIONAL)

Cast on 14 sts. Slipping first st of each row as if to purl, work in Garter Stitch, for 18 1/2 (20 1/2, 22 1/2, 24 1/2, 26 1/2, 28 1/2)" [47 (52, 57, 62, 67.5, 72.5) cm]. Bind off.

## FINISHING

Sew shoulder seams. Sew in Sleeves. Sew side seams, inserting belt into side seams at desired location, and turning back cuff.

## FRONT BANDS AND COLLAR

**Note** The Front Bands and Collar are worked in one piece.
Cast on 8 sts.

**Row 1** (WS) Knit.

**Row 2** Slip 1 as if to purl, knit to end. Repeat these 2 rows until piece measures same as Front to neck shaping, ending with a RS row.

**Inc Row for collar (WS)** K 1, knit into front and back of next st, knit to end. Continuing to slip first st every RS row, repeat Inc Row every 4th row until there are 32 (32, 33, 34, 35, 35) sts on needles. Work Rows 1 and 2 for 6 (6 1/2, 7, 8, 8 1/2, 8 3/4)" [15 (16.5, 18, 20.5, 21.5, 22) cm], ending with a RS row.

**Dec Row for collar (WS)** K 1, k2tog, knit to end. Continuing to slip first st every RS row, repeat Dec Row every 4th row until 8 sts remain. Work Rows 1 and 2 until piece measures same as corresponding section at beg of Band. Bind off. Using invisible seam (see Techniques, page 188), sew Bands and Collar to Front and neck edges, fitting curved side into neck. Sew buttons onto Left Front Band. Mark these positions on Right Band.

**Buttonholes** With RS facing, beg at bottom of Right Band, join yarn and work 1 sc in each selvage st to first button position; *ch 7, skip 6 sts, sc to next button position; repeat from * to last button position, ch 7, skip 6 sts, 2 sc. Fasten off. Weave in ends.

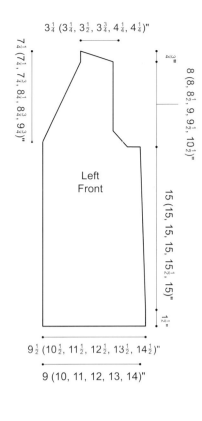

3 1/4 (3 1/4, 3 1/2, 3 3/4, 4 1/4, 4 1/4)"

7 1/4 (7 1/4, 7 1/4, 8 1/4, 8 1/4, 9 1/4)"

3/4"

8 (8, 8 1/2, 9, 9 1/2, 10 1/2)"

Left Front

15 (15, 15, 15, 15 1/2, 15)"

1 1/2"

9 1/2 (10 1/2, 11 1/2, 12 1/2, 13 1/2, 14 1/2)"

9 (10, 11, 12, 13, 14)"

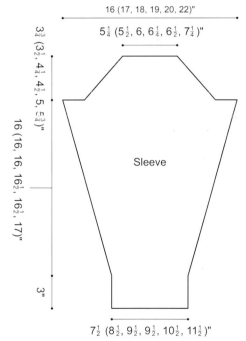

16 (17, 18, 19, 20, 22)"

5 1/4 (5 1/2, 6, 6 1/4, 6 1/2, 7 1/4)"

3 3/4 (3 1/2, 4, 4 1/2, 5, 5 3/4)"

16 (16, 16, 16 1/2, 16 1/2, 17)"

Sleeve

3"

7 1/2 (8 1/2, 9 1/2, 9 1/2, 10 1/2, 11 1/2)"

# The Cutaway Coat

## SIZES

S (M, L)

**Finished chest, buttoned** 36 3/4 (41, 45 1/2)" [93.5 (104, 115.5) cm]

**Length** 28 (29, 29 3/4)" [71 (73.5, 75.5) cm]

**Note** Before beginning pattern, circle all numbers pertaining to your size for ease in working.

## MATERIALS

(4) LION BRAND Wool-Ease

*3 oz (85 g) 197 yd (180 m) Ball*

*80% Acrylic, 20% Wool*

- 6 (6, 7) balls #152 Oxford Grey (MC) or color of your choice

(5) LION BRAND Lion Suede

*3 oz (85 g) 122 yd (110 m) Ball*

*100% Polyester*

- 1 skein #153 Ebony (CC) or color of your choice
- Size J-10 (6 mm) crochet hook OR SIZE TO OBTAIN GAUGE
- Size I-9 (5.5 mm) crochet hook
- Size H-8 (5 mm) crochet hook OR SIZE TO OBTAIN GAUGE
- Size G-6 (4 mm) crochet hook
- Scraps of contrasting yarn to be used as markers
- Large-eyed, blunt needle
- Needle and thread to match CC for sewing Frog
- Straight pins

## GAUGE

11 sts + 9 rows = 4" (10 cm) in pattern with MC on largest hook.

13 sc + 16 rows = 4" (10 cm) on second-smallest hook.

BE SURE TO CHECK YOUR GAUGE.

At once evening-worthy elegant and downtown fun and funky, this clever coat proves that a little drama goes a long way. Crocheted in a versatile dress-it-up-or-down gray and accented with rich black chenille and handworked frog closures, it's a knockout—not to mention tangible proof that some things just get better with age.

## CROCHET **EXPERIENCED**

NOTE Coat is made in one piece from the neck down.

## PATTERN STITCHES

**Pattern Row 1** Ch 1, sc in first dc, [dc in next sc, sc in next dc] across, ending dc in last sc, sc in top of t-ch; turn.

**Pattern Row 2** Ch 3, skip first sc, [sc in next dc, dc in next sc] across; turn.

## YOKE

**Note** Increases in pattern form raglan shaping.

With MC and largest hook, ch 28 (30, 32).

**Row 1 (RS)** Sc in 4th ch from hook, [dc in next ch, sc in next ch] 12 (13, 14) times, dc in same ch as last sc; turn—27 (29, 31) sts.

**Row 2** Ch 1, sc in first dc, 7 dc in next sc, [sc in next dc, dc in next sc] 2 times, sc in next dc, 7 dc in next sc, [sc in next dc, dc in next sc] 5 (6, 7) times, sc in next dc, 7 dc in next sc, [sc in next dc, dc in next sc] 2 times, sc in next dc, 7 dc in next sc, sc in top of t-ch; turn—51 (53, 55) sts. Mark center (4th) dc in each of four corners. Move markers up as you work each corner.

**Row 3** Ch 3, skip first sc, sc in next dc, dc in next dc, sc in next dc, *3 dc in marked dc, [sc in next st, dc in next st] across to next marker; repeat from * 2 more times, 3 dc in marked dc, sc in next dc, dc in next dc, sc in next dc, dc in last sc; turn—59 (61, 63) sts.

**Row 4 (beg neck inc)** Ch 3, sc in first dc, work in pattern as established, working 3 dc in marked corners, ending with (sc, dc) in top of t-ch; turn—69 (71, 73) sts.

**Row 5** Ch 1, sc in first dc, work in pattern as established, working 3 dc in marked corners, ending with sc in top of t-ch; turn—77 (79, 81) sts.

**Row 6** Ch 3, skip first sc, sc in next dc, work in pattern as established, working 3 dc in marked corners, ending with dc in last sc; turn—85 (87, 89) sts.

**Rows 7–12** Repeat Rows 4–6 twice—137 (139, 141) sts.

**Size Small**

**Rows 13–14** Repeat Rows 56—153 sts.

**Rows 15–16** Work Pattern Rows 1–2.

**Size Medium**

**Rows 13–16** Repeat Rows 4–6, then Row 5 once more—173 sts.

**Rows 17–18** Work Pattern Row 2, then Pattern Row 1.

**Size Large**

**Rows 13–18** Repeat Rows 4–6 twice—193 sts.

**Rows 19–20** Work Pattern Rows 1–2.

## BODY

**Row 1 (joining row) (RS)** Work 19 (22, 25) sts in pattern across Front, sc in marked corner dc, ch 5 for underarm, skip 35 (39, 43) arm sts, sc in marked corner dc, work in pattern for 41 (47, 53) sts across Back, sc in marked corner dc, ch 5 for underarm, skip 35 (39, 43) arm sts, sc in marked corner dc, work 19 (22, 25) sts in pattern across Front; turn—93 (105, 117) sts.

**Row 2** Work even in pattern, working one st into each ch at underarms.

**Rows 3–8** Work even in pattern.

**Row 9 (Dec Row)** Work 20 (23, 26) sts in pattern, dc2tog, place marker and sc in next st, dc2tog, work in pattern to 25 (28, 31) sts from end, dc2tog, place marker and sc in next st, dc2tog, work 20 (23, 26) sts in pattern to end; turn—89 (101, 113) sts.

**Rows 10–13** Work even in pattern, moving markers.

**Row 14** [Work in pattern to 2 sts before marked st, dc2tog, sc in marked st, dc2tog] twice, work in pattern to end—85 (97, 109) sts.

**Rows 15–18** Work even in pattern, moving markers.

**Rows 19–23** Repeat Rows 14–18—81 (93, 105) sts.

Fasten off.

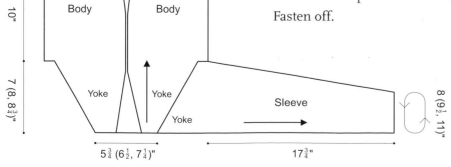

33¾ (38, 42½)"

25¾ (29½, 33)"

8"

Skirt        Skirt

Body Trim

1½"

10"

Body        Body

7 (8, 8¾)"

Yoke    Yoke        Sleeve        8 (9½, 11)"

Yoke

5¾ (6½, 7¼)"            17¾"

Change to second-smallest hook. With RS facing and MC, join with slip stitch to first st of lower edge. Ch 1, sc in first st, sc across lower edge, increasing 16 (18, 20) sc evenly spaced, 3 sc in last st of lower edge for corner; work 58 (61, 64) sc up Front; sc in 25 (27, 29) spare loops of neck, inc 5 sc evenly spaced; work 58 (61, 64) sc down Front; 2 sc in same st as beg, join with slip stitch to beg sc—247 (269, 291) sc. Fasten off.

## SLEEVES

With RS facing, MC, and largest hook, join with slip stitch in center (3rd) spare loop of ch-5 at underarm.

**Round 1** Ch 3, sc in next spare loop, dc in next spare loop, sc in same dc as joined, work in pattern across 35 (39, 43) arm sts, sc in same dc as joined, dc in next spare loop, sc in next spare loop; join with slip stitch to top of beg ch; turn—42 (46, 50) sts.

**Round 2** Ch 1, [dc in next sc, sc in next dc] around; join with slip stitch to beg ch; turn.

**Round 3 (dec round)** Ch 1, dc2tog, work in pattern to last 2 sts, dc2tog; join with slip stitch to beg ch; turn—40 (44, 48) sts.

**Round 4** Ch 3, work even in pattern; join with slip stitch to top of beg ch; turn.

**Round 5** Ch 1, work even in pattern; join with slip stitch to beg ch; turn.

**Rounds 6–17** Repeat Rounds 3–5 four times—32 (36, 40) sts.

**Rounds 18–40** Work [Rounds 3–5, then Rounds 4–5] four times, then Rounds 3–5 once more—22 (26, 30) sts. Change to second-smallest hook. With RS facing, sc around end of Sleeve, increasing 5 sc evenly spaced—27 (31, 35) sc. Fasten off. Weave in ends and block before adding Trim and Skirt.

## BODY TRIM

With RS facing, using CC and second-smallest hook, join with slip stitch to sc at center back of lower edge.

**Round 1** Ch 1, sc in same sc, sc around entire outside of piece, working 3 sc in lower Front corners; join with slip st to top of beg sc; turn.

**Round 2 (WS)** Ch 1, skip slip stitch, sc in next sc and in each sc around, working 3 sc in lower Front corners; join with slip stitch to top of beg sc. Fasten off. With RS facing, join MC.

**Rounds 3–5** Work Rounds 1–2, but do not fasten off; turn and repeat Round 2. Fasten off. With RS facing, join CC.

**Rounds 6–7** Work Rounds 1–2. Fasten off.

## SLEEVE TRIM

With CC and second-smallest hook, join in same sc as fastened. Work 7 rounds Trim as for Body.

## SKIRT

**Note** Hook size is gradually increased to loosen gauge.

**Row 1** With RS facing, using MC and second-smallest hook, skip center sc of corner of lower Body Trim, skip next 16 (18, 20) sc, join with slip stitch in next sc. Ch 1, sc in same sc, sc in next 80 (90, 100) sc; turn—81 (91, 101) sc. Leave 16 (18, 20) sc and center sc of other corner unworked.

**Row 2** Work Pattern Row 1.

**Row 3** Change to second-largest hook. Work Pattern Row 2.

**Row 4 (dec row)** Ch 2, dc in next sc, work in pattern across, ending dc2tog (last sc with top of turning chain); turn—79 (89, 99) sts.

**Rows 5–6** Work Pattern Rows 1–2.

**Rows 7–18** Change to largest hook. Repeat Rows 4–6 four times—71 (81, 91) sts. Fasten off.

## SKIRT TRIM

With RS facing, using MC and second-smallest hook, join with slip stitch in last unworked sc of lower Body Trim to right of Skirt.

**Row 1** Ch 1, sc in each sc edge row and 2 sc in each dc edge row along shaped side of Skirt; work 3 sc for corner; sc across lower edge, increasing 13 (15, 17) sc evenly spaced; 3 sc for corner in last st of lower edge; sc as before along other shaped side; slip stitch in first unworked sc of Body Trim. Fasten off. With RS facing and CC, join in last unworked sc of lower Body Trim to right of Skirt.

**Row 2** Ch 1, sc in each sc around Skirt, working 3 sc in corners; slip stitch in next 2 unworked sc of Body Trim; turn.

**Row 3 (WS)** Skip slip stitches, sc in each sc around Skirt, working 3 sc in corners; slip stitch in next unworked sc of Body Trim. Fasten off. With RS facing, join MC.

**Rows 4–6** Repeat Rows 2–3, but do not fasten off; slip stitch in one more unworked sc of Body Trim; turn and work Row 3 once more. Fasten off. With RS facing, join CC.

**Rows 7–8** Repeat Rows 2–3.

## FROG LOOPS—MAKE 3

**Note** Frogs should be made firmly. Join but do not turn at ends of rounds.

With CC and smallest hook, ch 5; join with slip st to form ring.

**Round 1** Ch 3, dc in ring, [ch 6, 3 dc in ring] 3 times, ch 6, dc in ring; join with slip stitch to top of beg ch—4 ch-6 spaces.

**Round 2** [Ch 1, (sc, hdc, 7 dc, hdc, sc) in next ch-6 space, ch 1, skip next dc, slip st in next dc] 3 times. Slip stitch in next dc, slip stitch in 6 ch of ch-6, slip stitch in next dc; join with slip stitch to top of beg sc. Fasten off. Weave in ends.

## BUTTONS—MAKE 3

**Note** Buttons should be made firmly. Join but do not turn at ends of rounds.

With CC and smallest hook, ch 5; join with slip stitch to form ring.

**Round 1** Ch 3, dc in ring, [ch 6, 3 dc in ring] 3 times, ch 6, slip stitch in 4th ch from hook for ch-3 ring, slip stitch in next 2 ch for stem, slip stitch in dc at base of ch, dc in ring; join with slip stitch to top of beg ch-3.

**Round 2** [Ch 1, (sc, hdc, 7 dc, hdc, sc) in next ch-6 space, ch 1, skip next dc, slip st in next dc] 3 times. Slip stitch in next dc, slip stitch in 3 sts of stem, slip stitch in ch-3 ring.

**Note** Work next 3 rounds in ch-3 ring.

**Round 3** Ch 1, 6 sc in ring, keeping Stem to back of work; join with slip stitch to top of beg sc.

**Round 4** Ch 1, 2 sc in each of next 6 sc; join with slip stitch to top of beg sc.

**Round 5** Ch 1, sc2tog 6 times; join with slip stitch to top of beg sc2tog. Fasten off, leaving long tail for finishing.

## FINISHING

Gather button by weaving tail through last round. Weave in ends. Button together 3 sets of frogs. Position and pin on Coat Front; when coat is closed, edges of trim should just meet. With needle and matching thread, sew frogs to coat, whip stitch around entire edge to secure, and reinforce at base of loop and stem of button.

# The Look-Back Jacket

Admiring looks coming and going are what most of us crave. This playful take on the tailored coat makes an entrance and leaves them wanting more. The original was in a classic—albeit somewhat staid—navy with white angora trim. We spiced it up with rich color and trimmed it with textural multi-tonal yarn for a more relaxed, fashion-forward effect.

## CROCHET INTERMEDIATE

BE SURE TO CHECK YOUR GAUGE.

NOTE For the body of this garment, three Flaps (2 Front, 1 Back) are worked separately, then joined. The body is then worked in one piece to the underarm. The Fronts and the Back are again worked separately to the shoulders. Note that the Flap openings fall to the back of the garment, not directly below the center underarm.

## SIZES

S (M, L, 1X, 2X)

**Finished chest, buttoned** 40 1/2 (44 3/4, 47 1/4, 49, 54 1/2)" [103 (113.5, 120, 124.5, 138.5) cm]

**Length** 32 1/4 (32 3/4, 33 1/4, 33 3/4, 34 1/4)" [82 (83, 84.5, 85.5, 87) cm]

**Note** Before beginning pattern, circle all numbers pertaining to your size for ease in working.

## MATERIALS

**[4]** LION BRAND Wool-Ease

*3 oz (85 g) 197 yd (180 m) Ball*

*80% Acrylic, 20 % Wool*

- 8 (9, 9, 10, 10) balls #179 Chestnut Heather (MC)
  or color of your choice

**[5]** LION BRAND Color Waves

*3 oz (85 g) 125 yd (113 m) Skein*

*83% Acrylic, 17% Polyester*

- 2 (3, 3, 3, 4) skeins #313 Sunset Red (CC)
  or color of your choice
- Sizes H-8 and K-10.5 (5 and 6.5 mm) crochet hooks OR SIZE TO OBTAIN GAUGE
- Six 1" (25 mm) buttons
- Large-eyed, blunt needle

## GAUGE

13 sts + 12 rows = 4" (10 cm) in Flat Knot Stitch with MC on larger hook.

13 sc + 16 rows = 4" (10 cm) with MC on smaller hook.

10 sc + 10 rows = 4" (10 cm) with CC on larger hook.

## PATTERN STITCH

**FLAT KNOT STITCH (multiple of 2 sts + 1)**

**Set-up row** Sc in 2nd ch from hook, *dc in next ch, sc in next ch; repeat from * across; turn.

**Row 1** Ch 1, *sc in sc of previous row, dc in dc of previous row; repeat from * across, ending sc in sc of previous row; turn. Repeat Row 1 for Flat Knot Stitch.

## BODY

**Back Flap** With MC and larger hook, ch 50 (56, 60, 66, 72). Work in Flat Knot Stitch for 19 rows—49 (55, 59, 65, 71) sts. Set piece aside.

**Left Front Flap** With MC and larger hook, ch 32 (36, 38, 38, 44). Work in Flat Knot Stitch for 12 rows—31 (35, 37, 37, 43) sts. Inc one st at beg of every RS row and end of every WS row 7 times total—38 (42, 44, 44, 50) sts. Set piece aside.

**Right Front Flap** Work as for Left Front Flap, but inc one st at end of every RS row and beg of every WS row 7 times total—38 (42, 44, 44, 50) sts.

**Join for body** With RS facing, work in pattern across Right Front, Back, and Left Front flaps—125 (139, 147, 153, 171) sts. Work even in pattern until Body measures 15" (38 cm) from join, or desired length to under-

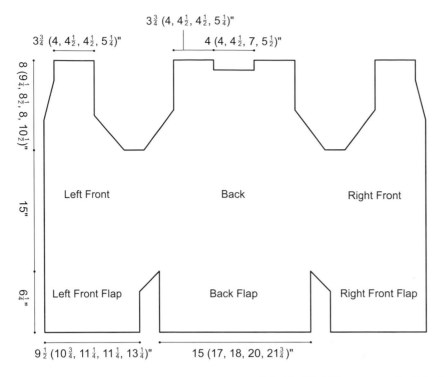

Diagram labels:
$3\frac{3}{4}$ $(4, 4\frac{1}{2}, 4\frac{1}{2}, 5\frac{1}{4})$"

$3\frac{3}{4}$ $(4, 4\frac{1}{2}, 4\frac{1}{2}, 5\frac{1}{4})$"

$4$ $(4, 4\frac{1}{2}, 7, 5\frac{1}{2})$"

$8$ $(9\frac{1}{4}, 8\frac{1}{2}, 8, 10\frac{1}{2})$"

15"

$6\frac{1}{4}$"

Left Front     Back     Right Front

Left Front Flap     Back Flap     Right Front Flap

$9\frac{1}{2}$ $(10\frac{3}{4}, 11\frac{1}{4}, 11\frac{1}{4}, 13\frac{1}{4})$"     $15$ $(17, 18, 20, 21\frac{3}{4})$"

arm, ending with a WS row.

**Right Front** Work across 28 (32, 34, 33, 39) sts; turn. Work 1 row. Dec one st at armhole edge every other row 10 (12, 11, 9, 13) times. AT THE SAME TIME, when armhole measures $2\frac{1}{2}$ $(2\frac{1}{2}, 2\frac{1}{2}, 2\frac{1}{2}, 3)$" [6.5 (6.5, 6.5, 6.5, 7.5) cm] from beg of shaping, dec one st at neck edge every other row 6 (7, 8, 9, 9) times—12 (13, 15, 15, 17) sts remain. Work even until armhole measures $8\frac{1}{2}$ $(9, 9\frac{1}{2}, 10, 10\frac{1}{2})$" [21.5 (23, 24, 25, 26) cm]. Fasten off.

**Back** With RS facing, skip 6 (6, 6, 8, 8) sts, then work 57 (63, 67, 71, 77) sts; turn. Dec one st at each end every other row 10 (12, 11, 9, 13) times—37 (39, 45, 53, 51) sts remain. Work even until armhole measures $7\frac{1}{2}$ (8, $8\frac{1}{2}$, 9, $9\frac{1}{2}$)" [19 (20.5, 21.5, 23, 24) cm] from beg of shaping.

**Shoulders and back neck** Work across 12 (13, 15, 15, 17) sts; turn. Work even on these sts for 1" (2.5 cm). Fasten off. Work second shoulder to match.

**Left Front** With RS facing, skip 6 (6, 6, 8, 8) sts, then work in pattern to end. Work as for Right Front.

### SLEEVES

With MC and larger hook, ch 30 (32, 32, 34, 36). Work in Flat Knot Stitch, inc one st at each end every 4th row 0 (1, 6, 11, 11) times; every 5th row 7 (8, 4, 0, 0) times; and every 6th row 1 (0, 0, 0, 0) times—45 (49, 51, 55, 57) sts. Work even until piece measures $15\frac{1}{4}$ $(15\frac{1}{2}, 15\frac{1}{2}, 15\frac{3}{4}, 15\frac{3}{4})$" [38.5 (39.5, 39.5, 40, 40) cm].

**Shape cap** Work to last 3 (3, 3, 4, 4) sts on next 2 rows; turn—39 (43, 45, 47, 49) sts remain. Dec one st at each end every row 3 (3, 3, 4, 5) times; every other row 8 (9, 10, 9, 7) times; then every row 3 (3, 3, 4, 5) times—11 (13, 13, 13, 15) sts remain. Fasten off.

**Cuffs** With CC and larger hook, work 29 (31, 31, 33, 35) sc across bottom of Sleeve. Work even in sc for $3\frac{1}{2}$" (9 cm), or desired length of turned back cuff. Fasten off.

## FINISHING

With MC, sew shoulder seams.

**Front bands** Mark positions for 4 evenly spaced buttonholes along Left Front, placing top button about 11" (28 cm) from top of Front. With MC and smaller hook, work 3 rows of sc up one Front, around the neck, and down the other Front.

**Next row** Sc to first buttonhole marker, ch 2, skip 2 sts (buttonhole made), *sc to next marker, make buttonhole; repeat from * 2 more times, sc to end. Work 3 more rows sc, working 2 sc into each ch-2 space. Fasten off.

**Back Flap border** With CC and larger hook, work 6 rows sc along bottom edge of Back.

**Left Front Flap border** With CC and larger hook, and beg at Front band, sc across Left Front, work 3 sc in corner, then sc to slanted edge. Ch 1; turn.

**Next row** Work sc into next row of slanted edge, sc to corner, work 3 sc in corner, sc to Front band. Repeat these two rows 2 more times. Fasten off.

**Right Front Flap border** Work as for Left Front Flap border.

## COLLAR

With CC and larger hook, ch 21. Work 16 (17, 19, 19, 21) rows sc.

**Next row** Work 18 sc, turn and work back. Dec one st at end of next row, then every other row 7 times—10 sts remain. Work 2 rows even. Fasten off.

**Second side of collar** Attach CC to beg of Collar at foundation ch and, working in opposite direction, work 16 (17, 19, 19, 21) rows sc. Work 18 sc, turn and work back. (Unworked sts should be at same edge of Collar as first side.) Dec one st at end of next row, then every other row 7 times —10 sts remain. Work 2 rows even. Fasten off. Attach shaped edge of Collar to neckline, with center tab section tucked inside neckband and sewn in place.

## BELT

With CC and larger hook, ch 41 (45, 48, 53, 58). Work 10 rows sc. Fasten off.

**Side ovals—Make 2** With MC and smaller hook, ch 15. Work 5 rows sc, then dec one st at beg and end of next 3 rows—8 sts. Work 1 row sc all around, working 3 sc in each corner. Fasten off. Attach each end of belt to oval section at 2nd row of sc. Sew buttons to oval sections, sewing through belt. Attach oval sections to Back of sweater just above Back Flaps (see archival picture). With MC, sew in Sleeves. Sew Sleeve seams. Weave in ends.

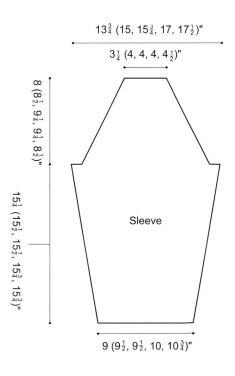

$13\frac{3}{4}$ (15, $15\frac{3}{4}$, 17, $17\frac{1}{2}$)"

$3\frac{1}{4}$ (4, 4, 4, $4\frac{1}{2}$)"

8 ($8\frac{1}{2}$, $9\frac{1}{4}$, $9\frac{1}{4}$, $8\frac{1}{2}$)"

$15\frac{1}{4}$ ($15\frac{1}{2}$, $15\frac{1}{2}$, $15\frac{3}{4}$, $15\frac{3}{4}$)"

Sleeve

9 ($9\frac{1}{2}$, $9\frac{1}{2}$, 10, $10\frac{3}{4}$)"

# The Romantic Cardigan

Originally designed as a discreet cover-up for one's dishabille, the Breakfast Jacket—as this sweet piece was originally named—is reincarnated as a flirty, feminine spring sweater, perfect for pairing with pretty dresses and soft, flowing skirts. The lacy shell pattern takes a slight bit of skill; microfiber yarn gives it a lovely sheen and a decadent feel.

## CROCHET INTERMEDIATE

### SIZES

S/M (L/XL)

**Finished chest** 40 (44)" [101.5 (112) cm]
**Note** Before beginning pattern, circle all numbers pertaining to your size for ease in working.

### MATERIALS

**(3)** LION BRAND Microspun
*2¹/₂ oz (70g) 168 yd (154 m) Ball*
*100% Microfiber Acrylic*

- 5 (6) balls #098 French Vanilla or color of your choice
- Size H-8 (5 mm) crochet hook OR SIZE TO OBTAIN GAUGE
- Scraps of contrasting yarn to be used as markers

### GAUGE

14 sts + 9 rows = 4" (10 cm) in pattern.
BE SURE TO CHECK YOUR GAUGE.

**NOTES** Jacket is worked from the neck down in one piece, a shaped triangle with increases at Fronts and Center Back. An underarm side seam (positioned slightly to the back) forms the "Sleeves." The stitch pattern is a RS row of Puff Stitches alternating with a WS row of decreases. Work decreases into the top of each Puff and into the chain (not in the chain-space) of previous row.

### STITCH EXPLANATIONS

**Puff (hdc2tog)** (Yarn over, insert hook in next st, draw up a loop) twice, yarn over and draw through all 5 loops on hook.
**Inc PUFF** (Puff, ch 1, Puff) all in same center back ch2-space.
**Puff Over Ch** Yarn over, insert hook in 2nd chain from hook, draw up a loop, yarn over, insert hook in 3rd chain from hook, draw up a loop, yarn over and draw through all 5 loops on hook.
**Shell** (2 dc, ch 2, 2 dc) all in same stitch.
**Inc Shell** (3 dc, ch 2, 3 dc) all in same center back ch-space.
**Fan** (Tr, ch 2, tr, ch 2, tr, ch 2, tr) all in same ch-space.

### JACKET

Ch 116.

**Row 1 (WS)** 2 dc in 6th ch from hook, dc in next 54 ch, Inc Shell in next ch, dc in next 54 ch, 3 dc in last ch; turn.

**Row 2 (RS)** Ch 3, Puff Over Ch, ch 1, Puff over first 2 dc, ch 1, (Puff, ch 1) 29 times across to center ch-2 space, Inc Puff in ch-2 space, ch 1, (Puff, ch 1) 29 times across, Puff over last dc and 4th ch of t-ch, ch 1, Puff in 3rd ch of turning chain; turn—64 Puffs.

**Row 3** Ch 5, 2 dc in first Puff, (dc in next ch, dc in next Puff) across to center, Inc Shell in center ch-space, (dc in next Puff, dc in next ch) across to last Puff, 3 dc in last Puff; turn.

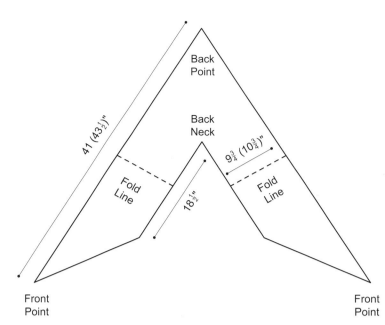

Back Point

Back Neck

41 (43½)"

9¾ (10¾)"

Fold Line

18½"

Fold Line

Front Point

Front Point

**Row 4** Ch 3, Puff Over Ch, ch 1, Puff over first 2 dc, ch 1, (Puff, ch 1) across to center ch-2 space, inc Puff in ch-2 space, ch 1, (Puff, ch 1) across to last dc, Puff over last dc and 4th ch of t-ch, ch 1, Puff in 3rd ch of t-ch; turn—72 Puffs. Repeat Rows 3–4 for 9 (10) more times, increasing 8 Puffs every 2 rows—total 144 (152) Puffs. Fasten off.

## FINISHING

**Seam for sleeves** From Left Front point, counting along the last row made, skip 18 Puffs, mark the next ch-1. From the Center Back point, skip 18 Puffs, mark the next ch-1. Repeat for Right Front and in other direction from Back point. With RS together, fold triangle so Front points meet Center Back point, matching markers on each side. Join at marker and slip stitch in next 15 (17) sts (working away from the points), matching sts and working through both thicknesses. Fasten off. Seam second side as for first.

## BORDER

**Round 1** With RS facing, join with slip stitch in ch-2 space at center back point, ch 1, sc in same space, (sc in next Puff, sc in next ch) 17 times, sc in next Puff, sc2tog (same 2 sts as joined for seam), (sc in next Puff, sc in next ch) 17 times, 2 sc in last Puff, work 55 (61) sc evenly spaced along pattern row edges up Right Front, sc in 111 spare loops of foundation ch at neck, 55 (61) sc down pattern row edges of Left Front, 2 sc in first Puff of lower edge, sc along lower edge, ending sc in last Puff, slip stitch in beg sc; turn—366 (378) sc.

**Round 2** Ch 3, skip slip stitch (skip next 2 sc, Shell in next sc, skip next 2 sc, dc in next sc) around, working (dc, ch 3, dc) in each Front lower corner, ending dc in same sc as beg, ch 1, sc in top of beg ch; turn.

**Round 3** Ch 3, dc in same space, (Shell in ch-space of next Shell, skip 2 dc of Shell, dc in next lone dc) around, working Shell in ch-3 space of Front corners, ending 2 dc in same space as beg, ch 1, sc in top of beg ch; turn.

**Round 4** Ch 6, tr in same space, ch 2, (skip 2 dc of Shell, sc in next lone dc, ch 2, Fan in ch-space of next Shell, ch 2) around, ending sc in last lone dc, ch 2, (tr, ch 2, tr) in same space as beg, ch 1, sc in 4th ch of beg ch; turn.

**Round 5** Ch 2, Puff in same space, ch 3, (Puff in next ch-2 space, ch 4, sc in next sc, ch 4, skip next ch-2 space, [Puff in next ch-2 space, ch 3] twice) around to last sc, sc in last sc, ch 4, skip next ch 2-space, Puff in next ch-2 space, ch 3, slip stitch in top of beg Puff.
Fasten off.

**Round 1** With RS facing, join with slip stitch at underarm seam. Sc2tog (same 2 sts as joined for seam), sc in 41 (53) sts around armhole; join with slip stitch in beg sc; turn—42 (54) sc.

**Round 2** Ch 3, skip slip stitch, (skip next 2 sc, Shell in next sc, skip next 2 sc, dc in next sc) 7 (9) times around, ending omit last dc; join with slip stitch to top of beg ch; turn.

**Rounds 3–4** Ch 3, (Shell in ch-space of next Shell, skip 2 dc of Shell, dc in next lone dc) around, ending omit last dc; join with slip stitch to top of beg ch; turn.

**Round 5** Ch 1, sc in same st, (ch 2, Fan in ch-space of next Shell, ch 2, skip 2 dc of Shell, sc in next lone dc) around, ending omit last sc; join with slip stitch in beg sc; do not turn.

**Round 6 (RS)** Ch 1, sc in same st, (ch 4, skip next ch-2 space, [Puff in next ch-2 space, ch 3] twice, Puff in next ch-2 space, ch 4, sc in next sc) around, ending omit last sc; join with slip stitch in beg sc.
Fasten off.

With RS facing, fold over edging along foundation ch at neck to outside for Collar. At end of neck, locate first unworked sc of Sleeve border Round 1. Join with slip stitch, ch 1, sc in same sc, [ch 1, without turning, work sc through front loop by inserting hook from top to bottom under front loop of previous sc] 48 times, or until Tie measures 18" (45.5 cm) or desired length. Fasten off. Work on second side as for first. Weave in ends. Lightly block or steam, particularly the lace border.

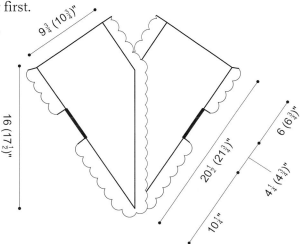

# CHAPTER 2

# Layering It On: Vests and Shrugs

As practical and sophisticated today as in decades past, vests and shrugs provided a light layer of warmth on days (or occasions) when a bulky coat or jacket just won't do. Most vintage vests have a tailored air to them, an attitude that you can either embrace wholeheartedly or soften up with a more casual choice of yarns and colors. Choose a more elegant fiber and they can double nicely as special-occasion tops.

Shrugs, of course, were invented as eveningwear, often worn to chase away the chill when wearing a bare-shouldered cocktail dress. And while a shrug remains a stylish choice for dinner and dancing, these modern interpretations are equally fashionable for the daylight hours.

These two great types of garments find common ground in one area that busy knitters and crocheters will appreciate: constructed in just one or two pieces, these projects finish up in a flash. That, of course, leaves time for other pursuits, or perhaps a more time-consuming sweater.

# The Shapely Vest

We vamped up this classic tailored vest by knitting it in sparkly metallic yarn. The result is an instant transformation from prim and proper to fun and flirty. Front darts give it a sexy, figure-flattering shape, perfect for pairing with trousers or a black velvet skirt.

## KNIT **INTERMEDIATE**

### SIZES

S (M, L, 1X)

**Finished chest, buttoned** 32½ (36, 39½, 43)" [82.5 (91.5, 100.5, 109) cm]

**Length** 17 (17, 18, 18)" [43 (43, 45.5, 45.5) cm]

**Note** Before beginning pattern, circle all numbers pertaining to your size for ease in working.

### MATERIALS

LION BRAND Glitterspun

1³/₄ oz (50g) 115 yd (105 m) Ball
60% Acrylic, 27% Cupro, 13% Polyester

- 6 (7, 8, 9) balls #135 Bronze or color of your choice
- Size 9 (5.5 mm) knitting needles OR SIZE TO OBTAIN GAUGE
- Stitch markers
- Stitch holders
- Seven ⁵/₈" (16 mm) buttons
- Large-eyed, blunt needle

### GAUGE

22 sts + 28 rows = 4" (10 cm) in Pattern Stitch.
BE SURE TO CHECK YOUR GAUGE.

**NOTE** Vest is worked in one piece from bottom of Back over shoulders to bottom of Fronts. Keep the first and last stitch of every row in Garter Stitch (knit every row). Work all increases in pattern.

### PATTERN STITCH

(multiple of 5 sts + 3)

**Row 1** (WS) Knit.

**Row 2** P 1, *k 1, p 4; repeat from * to last 2 sts, k 1, p 1.

**Rows 3, 5, and 7** *K 3, p 2; repeat from * to last 3 sts, k 3.

**Rows 4, 6, and 8** *P 1, k 1, p 1, k 2; repeat from * to last 3 sts, p 1, k 1, p 1.

### STITCH EXPLANATION

**sk2p**—Slip 1 as if to knit, knit 2 together, pass the slipped stitch over the knit two together stitches.

### BACK

Cast on 89 (99, 109, 119) sts using long tail cast on (see Techniques, page 188).

**Row 1 (WS)** *K 1, p 1; repeat from * to last st, k 1.

**Row 2** K 2, *p 1, k 1; repeat from * to last st, k 1.

Repeat these 2 rows of ribbing until piece measures 10" (25.5 cm), slightly stretched, ending with a WS row.

**Shape armholes (RS)** K 2, p 1, sk2p rib to last 6 sts, k3tog, p 1, k 2.

**Next row** Work in rib.

Repeat last 2 rows 1 (1, 2, 2) more times—81 (91, 97, 107) sts.

**Next row (RS)** K 2, p 1, ssk (see Techniques, page 188), rib to last 5 sts, k2tog, p 1, k 2.

**Next row** Work in rib.

Repeat last 2 rows 3 (3, 4, 3) more times—73 (83, 87, 99) sts.  Work even in rib until armhole measures 6½ (6½, 7½, 7½)" [16.5 (16.5, 19, 19) cm] from beg of shaping, ending with a WS row.

LEFT FRONT

Work 21 (26, 26, 31) sts in rib and place on holder. Bind off next 31 (31, 35, 37) sts in rib for neck, rib last 21 (26, 26, 31) sts.

**Begin Pattern Stitch (WS)** Rib 4, place marker,  work Row 1 of Pattern Stitch over 13 (18, 18, 23) sts, place marker, rib 4.

**Next row** Rib 4, work Row 2 of Pattern Stitch between markers, rib 4. Continue in pattern with rib on both ends for 2½" (6.5 cm), ending with a WS row.

**Next row (RS)** Rib 4, slip marker, M1L (see Techniques, page 188), work in pattern to last 4 sts, rib 4.

Inc at Front edge every RS row 9 more times, working inc into pattern and ending with a WS row—31 (36, 36, 41) sts.

**Next row** Rib 4, slip marker, M1L, work to last 4 sts, M1R (see Techniques, page 188  ), slip marker, rib 4.

Inc at Front edge every RS row 9 (9, 12, 12) more times and at armhole edge every RS row 9 (9, 11, 11) more times—51 (56, 61, 66) sts. Work even in pattern and rib until Front measures 10 (10, 10½, 10½)" [25.5 (25.5, 26.5, 26.5) cm], ending with a RS row.

**Set-up row for dart shaping (WS)** Rib 4, work 19 (24, 24, 29)  sts in pattern, place marker, work 24 (24, 29, 29) sts in pattern, rib 4.

**Next row (RS)** Work in pattern as established, dec one st before and after dart marker every 4th row 5 times—41 (46, 51, 56) sts. Remove marker and work even in pattern and rib edges until Front from armhole measures ½" (1.5 cm) less than Back, ending with a WS row.

**Shape Front bottom edge (RS)** Short Rows: Work to last 11 sts, slip next st to right needle, wrap yarn around slipped st and place st back on left needle; turn.

Work 1 row even in pattern.

**Next row** Work to 4 (5, 6, 7) sts before wrapped st, slip next st, wrap and slip back to left needle; turn.

Work 1 row even in pattern.

Repeat last 2 rows 4 more times, ending with a WS row—10 sts.

**Bottom edge ribbing (RS)** Work in ribbing across all stitches, knitting or purling wraps with each wrapped st—41 (46, 51, 56) sts. Work in rib for 4 rows. Bind off in rib.

**Button placement** Mark placement for 7 buttons with top button ¹/₂"
(1.5 cm) from last Front inc and bottom button ¹/₂" (1.5 cm) from
bottom edge.

### RIGHT FRONT

Place sts from holder onto needle. With WS facing, attach yarn and
work as for Left Front, reversing shaping. At same time, work buttonholes on RS rows opposite buttons by working to last 4 sts, ssk, yarn
over, k 2.

### FINISHING

Sew side seams. Sew on buttons. Weave in ends.

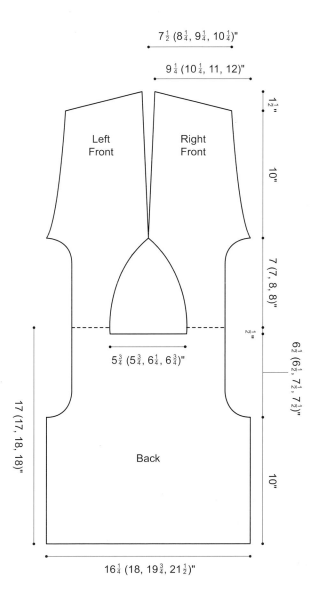

# The Hug-Me-Tight Shrug

Glittery, glamorous, and gorgeous; need we say more? Worked in a simple rib pattern with easy increases, this clever cover-up is simply two short takes on sleeves stitched together across the back. Shimmery yarn makes it an elegant choice for evening or a playful piece to pair with jeans and a tiny tank.

KNIT **EASY +**

### SIZES

S (M, L)

**To fit bust** 32–34 (36–38, 40–42)" [81.5–86.5 (91.5–96.5, 101.5–106.5) cm]

**Note** Before beginning pattern, circle all numbers pertaining to your size for ease in working.

### MATERIALS

**(4)** LION BRAND Glitterspun

*1³/₄ oz (50 g) 115 yd (105 m) Ball*

*60% Acrylic, 27% Cupro, 13% Polyester*

- 6 (7, 8) balls #170 Gold or color of your choice
- Sizes 7 and 9 (4.5 and 5.5 mm) 32" (80 cm) circular needles OR SIZE TO OBTAIN GAUGE
- Large-eyed, blunt needle

### GAUGE

22 sts + 28 rows = 4" (10 cm) in Pattern Stitch on larger needle.

BE SURE TO CHECK YOUR GAUGE.

### PATTERN STITCH

(multiple of 4 sts + 1)

**Row 1** K 2, *p 2, k 2; repeat from * to last 3 sts, p 3.

Repeat Row 1 for Pattern Stitch.

### SLEEVE AND BODY—MAKE 2

With smaller needle, cast on 47 (51, 55) sts using long tail cast on (see Techniques, page 188).

**Row 1** *K 1, p 1; repeat from * to last st, k 1.

**Row 2** *P 1, k 1; repeat from * to last st, p 1.

Repeat these 2 rows of ribbing until piece measures 3½" (9 cm), ending with Row 2.

**Inc row (RS)** Changing to larger needle, *k 1, M1 knit (see Techniques, page 188), p 1, M1 purl (see Techniques, page 188); repeat from * to last st, p 1—93 (101, 109) sts.

Work even in Pattern Stitch until piece measures 6 (6½, 7)" [15 (16.5, 18) cm], ending with a WS row.

**Inc row (RS)** K 2, *M1 purl, p 1, M1 knit, k 1; repeat from * to last 3 sts, p 3—181 (197, 213) sts.

Work even in Pattern Stitch until piece measures 12 (13, 14)" [30.5 (33, 35.5) cm] from beg. Bind off in pattern.

### FINISHING

Sew Sleeve seams. Sew Backs to each other, matching rib pattern, beg 3 (3½, 3½)" [7.5 (9, 9) cm] down from top, and sew for approximately 10 (10½, 11)" [25.5 (26.5, 28) cm]. (Sew more for a tighter fit and less for a looser fit.) Weave in ends.

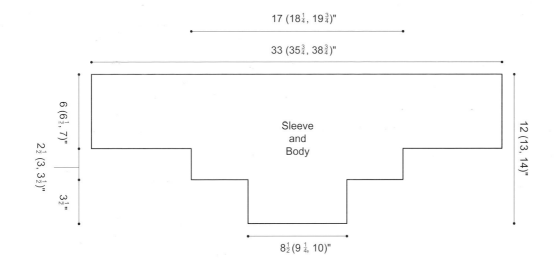

17 (18¼, 19¾)"

33 (35¾, 38¾)"

6 (6½, 7)"

2½ (3, 3½)"

3½"

Sleeve
and
Body

12 (13, 14)"

8½ (9¼, 10)"

# The Romance Bolero

This cute cropped jacket was originally devised as a romantic cocktail cover-up knit in a cloud of pastel mohair. It was sweet, but somewhat predictable. Searching for a more fashion-forward look, we decided to shake things up by reworking it in a fun and furry novelty yarn, and adding a single standout button to the front. Perfection!

KNIT with CROCHET edging **EASY +**

## SIZES

S (M, L, 1X, 2X)

**Finished chest** 38 1/4 (41 3/4, 45, 48, 53)"
[97 (106, 114.5, 122, 134.5) cm]

**Length** 16 1/4 (16 1/4, 17 1/4, 17 3/4, 18 1/4)"
[41.5 (41.5, 44, 45, 46.5) cm]

**Note** Before beginning pattern, circle all numbers pertaining to your size.

## MATERIALS

**(6)** LION BRAND Fancy Fur
*1 3/4 oz (50 g) 39 yd (35 m) Ball*
*55% Polyamide, 45% Polyester*

- 7 (9, 10, 11, 13) balls #253 Bold Black (MC)
  or color of your choice

**(4)** LION BRAND Glitterspun
*1 3/4 oz (50g) 115 yd (105 m) Ball*
*60% Acrylic, 27% Cupro, 13% Polyester*

- 1 ball #153 Onyx (CC)
  or color of your choice
- Size 13 (9 mm) knitting needles OR SIZE TO OBTAIN GAUGE
- Size K-10.5 (6.5 mm) crochet hook for edging
- Large-eyed, blunt needle

## GAUGE

10 sts + 14 rows = 4" (10 cm) in Stockinette stitch (knit on RS, purl on WS). BE SURE TO CHECK YOUR GAUGE.

## BACK

With MC, cast on 44 (48, 52, 56, 62) sts. Work in St st, inc one st each end every 8th row 2 times—48 (52, 56, 60, 66) sts. Work even until piece measures 6 1/2" (16.5 cm), ending with a WS row.

**Shape armholes** Bind off 4 (5, 5, 5, 6) sts at beg of next 2 rows. Dec one st each end every other row 3 (4, 5, 5, 6) times—34 (34, 36, 40, 42) sts. Work even until armhole measures 8 (8, 9, 9 1/2, 10)" [20.5 (20.5, 23, 24, 25.5) cm] from beg of shaping, ending with a WS row.

**Shape shoulders** Bind off 3 sts at beg of next 6 (6, 6, 4, 2) rows, then 4 sts at beg of next (0, 0, 2, 4) rows—16 (16, 18, 20, 20) sts. Bind off remaining sts for Back neck.

## LEFT FRONT

With MC, cast on 22 (24, 26, 28, 31) sts. Work in St st, inc one st at beg of every 4th RS row 2 times—24 (26, 28, 30, 33) sts. Work even until piece measures 6 1/2" (16.5 cm), ending with a WS row.

**Shape armhole** Bind off 4 (5, 5, 5, 6) sts at beg of next row. Dec one st at beg of every RS row 3 (4, 5, 5, 6) times—17 (17, 18, 20, 21) sts. Work even until armhole measures 6 (6, 7, 7 1/2, 7 1/2)" [15 (15, 18, 19, 19) cm] from beg of shaping, ending with a RS row.

**Shape neck** Bind off 5 (5, 6, 7, 7) sts at neck edge. Dec one st at neck edge every WS row 3 times—9 (9, 9, 10, 11) sts. Work even until armhole measures 8 (8, 9, 9 1/2, 10)" [20.5 (20.5, 23, 24, 25.5) cm], ending with a WS row.

**Shape shoulder** Bind off 3 sts at beg of next 3 (3, 3, 2, 1) RS rows, then 4 sts at beg of next (0, 0, 1, 2) RS rows.

## RIGHT FRONT

Work as for Left Front, reversing shaping.

## SLEEVES

With MC, cast on 30 (32, 34, 36, 38) sts. Work in St st, inc one st each end every other row 3 (6, 6, 6, 4) times, then every 3rd row 2 (0, 0, 0, 2) times—40 (44, 46, 48, 50) sts. Work even until piece measures $3^1/_2$ ($3^1/_2$, $3^1/_2$, $3^1/_2$, 4)" [9 (9, 9, 9, 10) cm], ending with a WS row.

**Shape Cap** Bind off 4 (5, 5, 5, 6) sts at beg of next 2 rows. Dec one st each end every row 4 (4, 4, 5, 1) times, then every other row 5 (5, 6, 6, 9) times—14 (16, 16, 16, 18) sts. Bind off.

## FINISHING

With CC, sew shoulder seams. Sew in Sleeves. Sew side and Sleeve seams.

**Edging** With RS facing, CC, and beg at right side seam, work 2 rows sc around entire Jacket, working 3 sc into each corner. Join with slip stitch to beg sc; turn. Work slip stitch into each sc around. Fasten off. Repeat edging for each Sleeve. Weave in ends.

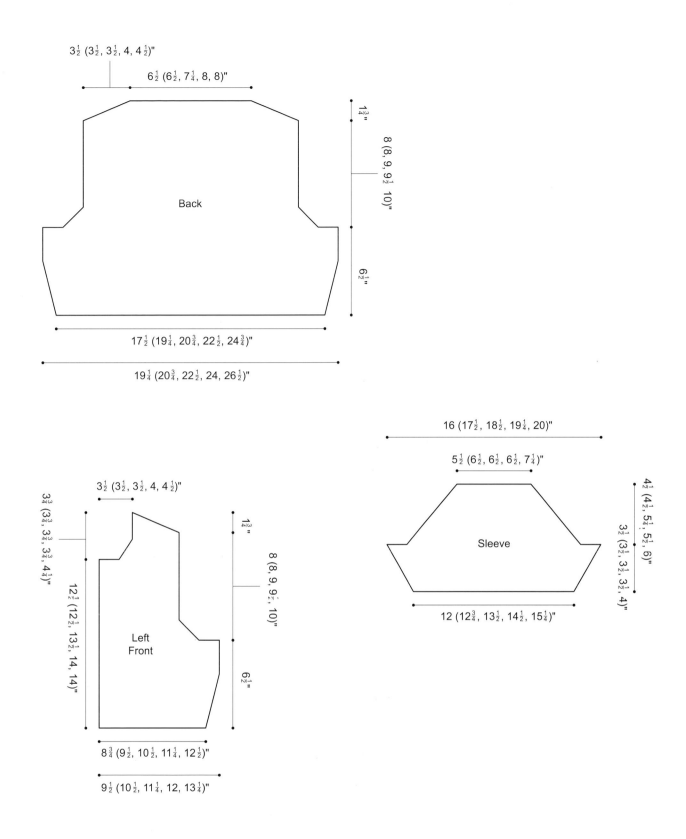

Back

$3\frac{1}{2}$ $(3\frac{1}{2}, 3\frac{1}{2}, 4, 4\frac{1}{2})$"

$6\frac{1}{2}$ $(6\frac{1}{2}, 7\frac{1}{4}, 8, 8)$"

$1\frac{3}{4}$"

$8$ $(8, 9, 9\frac{1}{2}, 10)$"

$6\frac{1}{2}$"

$17\frac{1}{2}$ $(19\frac{1}{4}, 20\frac{3}{4}, 22\frac{1}{2}, 24\frac{3}{4})$"

$19\frac{1}{4}$ $(20\frac{3}{4}, 22\frac{1}{2}, 24, 26\frac{1}{2})$"

Left Front

$3\frac{1}{2}$ $(3\frac{1}{2}, 3\frac{1}{2}, 4, 4\frac{1}{2})$"

$3\frac{3}{4}$ $(3\frac{3}{4}, 3\frac{3}{4}, 3\frac{3}{4}, 4\frac{1}{2})$"

$1\frac{3}{4}$"

$12\frac{1}{2}$ $(12\frac{1}{2}, 13\frac{1}{2}, 14, 14)$"

$8$ $(8, 9, 9\frac{7}{2}, 10)$"

$6\frac{1}{2}$"

$8\frac{3}{4}$ $(9\frac{1}{2}, 10\frac{1}{2}, 11\frac{1}{4}, 12\frac{1}{2})$"

$9\frac{1}{2}$ $(10\frac{1}{2}, 11\frac{1}{4}, 12, 13\frac{1}{4})$"

Sleeve

$16$ $(17\frac{1}{2}, 18\frac{1}{2}, 19\frac{1}{4}, 20)$"

$5\frac{1}{2}$ $(6\frac{1}{2}, 6\frac{1}{2}, 6\frac{1}{2}, 7\frac{1}{4})$"

$4\frac{1}{2}$ $(4\frac{1}{2}, 5\frac{1}{4}, 5\frac{1}{2}, 6)$"

$3\frac{1}{2}$ $(3\frac{1}{2}, 3\frac{1}{2}, 3\frac{1}{2}, 4)$"

$12$ $(12\frac{3}{4}, 13\frac{1}{2}, 14\frac{1}{2}, 15\frac{1}{4})$"

# The Retro Vest

We took this tastefully tailored vest and loosened it up a little by relaxing the fit and using tone-on-tone shades of tweedy wool. Instead of layering it over a stuffy shirt, we let the wide sweep of the shoulders serve as sleeves and present it as a travel-worthy top.

CROCHET **INTERMEDIATE +**

### SIZES

S (M, L, 1X)

**Finished chest, buttoned** 37 (41, 45, 49)" [94 (104, 114.5, 124.5) cm]

**Length** 18 3/4 (19 1/4, 20, 20 1/2)" [47.5 (49, 51, 52) cm]

**Note** Before beginning pattern, circle all numbers pertaining to your size for ease in working.

### MATERIALS

**(4)** LION BRAND Wool-Ease

*3 oz (85 g) 197 yd (180 m) Balls*

*80% Acrylic, 20% Wool*

- 3 (4, 5, 6) balls #403 Mushroom (MC)
- 1 ball #126 Chocolate Brown (CC) or colors of your choice
- Size J-10 (6 mm) crochet hook OR SIZE TO OBTAIN GAUGE
- Stitch markers
- Five 7/8" (22 mm) buttons

### GAUGE

14 sc + 16 rows = 4" (10 cm).

BE SURE TO CHECK YOUR GAUGE.

**NOTE** This vest is worked sideways, in two pieces, beginning at the armhole edge. Stitches are added at the side for a gusset until the piece reaches its final length. At the same time, the shoulders are shaped using increases in the center stitch. When the shoulders are complete, the V-neck Front and the Back are worked separately. A second piece is worked to match, then slip stitched to the first half at center Back. The Borders are added last.

### HALF BODY—MAKE 2

**Armhole** With MC, ch 64 (68, 72, 76).

**Row 1** Sc in 2nd ch from hook and in each ch across; join with slip stitch to beg sc; turn—63 (67, 71, 75) sts. Place marker in 32nd (34th, 36th, 38th) st (center st).

**Row 2** Ch 1, sc to center st, 2 sc in center st, sc to end; join with slip st to beg sc; turn—64 (68, 72, 76) sts.

**Rows 3, 5, and 7** Very loosely ch 5, sc into nub in back of each of the 5 ch, sc to end. Sc under both legs of V on other side of beg ch-5. (This forms the underarm gusset.) Turn—10 sts increased.

**Rows 4, 6, and 8** Very loosely ch 5, sc under both legs of V of each of the 5 ch, sc to center st, 2 sc in center st, sc to end, sc into nub in back of each beg ch as in row 3; turn—11 sts increased.

**Rows 10, 12, 14, and 16** Ch 1, sc to center st, 2 sc in center st, sc to end; turn—one st increased.

**Rows 9, 11, 13, 15, and 17** Ch 1, work even in sc; turn.

Shoulder is now complete—131 (135, 139, 143) sts.

**Front** Ch 1, sc 60 (62, 64, 66); turn, leaving remaining sts unworked.

**Shape V-neck** Sc2tog at neck edge every row 20 (16, 12, 8) times, then every other row 0 (4, 8, 12) times. AT THE SAME TIME, after working 14 (18, 22, 26) rows of V-neck, work 2 sc in last st (at bottom edge) every other row 3 times—43 (45, 47, 49) sts. Fasten off.

**Back** Join MC in center st. Work even in sc on 66 (68, 70, 72) sts for 20 (24, 28, 32) rows. Fasten off.

### FINISHING

With MC, join the two halves at center Back using slip stitch.

**Vest border** Mark positions for 5 evenly spaced buttonholes on Right Front edge. With CC and beg at Back Left neck, work 3 rounds of sc all around vest, working 3 sc in each outer corner and sc3tog at each inner corner to miter.

**Round 4 (buttonhole round)** *Work to buttonhole marker, ch 2, skip 2 sts; repeat from * to last marker, ch 2, skip 2 sts, sc to end of round. Work 3 more rounds sc, mitering corners. Fasten off.

**Armhole borders** With CC, work 2 rounds sc around each armhole. Fasten off.

Sew buttons opposite buttonholes. Weave in ends.

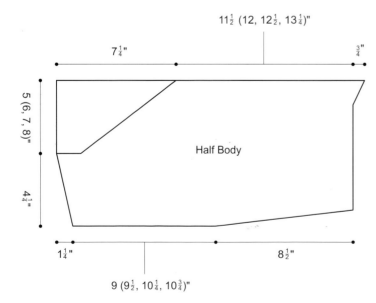

# The Poet Shrug

With its picot edge and pretty texture, this shawl with sleeves has a romantic look we love. Modern microfiber yarn gives the new version a softer, more supple drape than that of the original; the result is a beautiful piece, perfect for window shopping in the city or curling up on the couch with a good book.

CROCHET **EASY**

### SIZE

Length cuff-to-cuff 53″ (134.5 cm)
Width 26″ (66 cm)

### MATERIALS

(3) LION BRAND Microspun
*2¹/₂ oz (70 g) 168 yd (154 m) Ball*
*100% Microfiber Acrylic*

- 6 balls #149 Silver Grey
  or color of your choice
- Size I-9 (5.5 mm) crochet hook OR
  SIZE TO OBTAIN GAUGE
- Large-eyed, blunt needle

### GAUGE

14 sts + 14 rows = 4″ (10 cm) in Pattern Stitch.
BE SURE TO CHECK YOUR GAUGE.

**NOTE** Shrug is worked from cuff to cuff.

### SHRUG

Ch 91. Skip first ch, *sc in each of next 2 ch, dc in each of next 2 ch; repeat from * across, ending sc in last 2 ch; turn—90 sts.
**Pattern Row** Ch 1, sc into each sc and dc into back loop of each dc across; turn.
Repeat Pattern Row until piece measures 39″ (99 cm) or desired length.

### EDGING

Work Scallop edging along one long edge.
**Scallop edging** Ch 3, 2 dc in first st, *skip 2 sts, sc in next st, skip 2 sts, (3 dc, ch 3, 3 dc) in next st; repeat from * across, ending skip 2 sts, sc in next st, skip 2 sts, 3 dc in last st. Fasten off.
Join with slip st to corner of second long edge. Work Scallop edging along second long edge.

### CUFFS

Ch 27. Sc in 2nd ch from hook and in each ch across; turn—26 sts.
**Rib Pattern Row** Ch 1, sc into back loop of each sc across; turn.
Repeat Rib Pattern Row until piece measures 8¹/₂″ (21.5 cm) or desired Cuff width. Fasten off.

### FINISHING

Gather width of Shrug and tack to Cuffs. Sew on Cuffs. Sew Cuff seams. Weave in ends.

~~~~~~~~~~~~~~~~~~~~~~~~~~~~~~~~~~~~~~~~~~~~~~

# CHAPTER 3

# Under Wraps: Shawls and Wraps

Flash back to the Eisenhower era, when circle skirts and glamour girl dresses were topped with movie-star stoles or ultra-feminine shawls. Fast-forward to the present and you'll see that our passion for enveloping the shoulders in a bit of luxury hasn't waned in the least.

Creating one of these lasting bits of beauty is a surprisingly simple exercise. There's little sizing to be done with a shawl or scarf (almost any length or width will do), and today's selection of glitzy, glamorous yarns makes it easy to fashion something special using even the most basic of stitches.

~~~~~~~~~~~~~~~~~~~~~~~~~~~~~~~~~~~~~~~~~~~~~~

# The Wrap Star

The Sonntag, as this cleverly constructed piece was called, served to combat the chill of a poorly heated home on Sundays or other special occasions. Reworked in a graphic black-and-gray color combination, it takes on an edgy urban attitude and becomes a dramatic focal point for any ensemble.

KNIT with CROCHET edging **INTERMEDIATE**

## SIZE

**Width** at shoulder 32″ (81.5 cm)
**Length** 19″ (48.5 cm)

## MATERIALS

 LION BRAND Wool-Ease
*3 oz (85 g) 197 yd (180 m) Ball*
*80% Acrylic, 20% Wool*

- 3 balls #151 Grey Heather (MC)
- 2 balls #153 Black (CC)
  or colors of your choice
- Size 8 (5 mm) circular needle OR
  SIZE TO OBTAIN GAUGE
- Size H-8 (5 mm) crochet hook for
  edging
- About 1 yd (1 m) waste yarn
- Stitch holders
- Stitch markers
- Two 1″ (25 mm) buttons or two 25″
  (63.5 cm) lengths of ribbon, cord,
  tassel, or tie of choice

## GAUGE

20 sts + 28 rows = 4″ (10 cm) in pattern stitch. BE SURE TO CHECK YOUR GAUGE.

**NOTE** Work 2 selvage stitches at each end of row in Stockinette stitch (knit on RS, purl on WS). M1R and M1L (see Techniques, page 188) should be made in either knit or purl in pattern as established.

### SHAWL

With waste yarn and MC, work provisional cast-on (see Techniques, page 188) 21 sts for lower back.

**Row 1 (RS)** K 2 (selvage), p 2, k 3, p 7, k 3, p 2, k 2 (selvage).

**Row 2** P 2 (selvage), k 2, p 3, k 7, p 3, k 2, p 2 (selvage).

**Row 3** K 2, M1R (see Techniques, page 188), p 2, k 3, p 7, k 3, p 2, M1L, k 2.

**Row 4** Purl.

**Row 5** K 2, M1R, k 1, p 7, k 3, p 7, k 1, M1L, k 2.

**Row 6** P 4, k 7, p 3, k 7, p 4.

**Row 7** K 2, M1R, k 2, p 7, k 3, p 7, k 2, M1L, k 2.

**Row 8** Purl.

Continue in pattern as established, working 2 increases on each RS row and incorporating the increases into pattern (as in chart), until piece measures 15″ (38 cm) or desired length from lower back to back neck.

**Divide for neck** Work to center 21 sts, k 1, cast on 1 (for selvage), put center 19 sts on holder for neck; using second ball of MC, cast on 1, k 1 (for selvage), then work in pattern as established to end of row. Working both sides at same time and keeping 2-stitch selvage at neck edges, work even for 4″ (10 cm), ending with a WS row.

**Dec Row** K 2, work in pattern to 3 sts before neck opening, k2tog, k 1; on left shoulder, k 1, ssk (see Techniques, page 188), work in pattern to last 2 sts, k 2.

Work dec row every 4th row 4 more times, then every other row until 3 sts remain on each side. Bind off.

## BORDER

Remove provisional cast on and place lower back sts onto holder.
With RS facing and CC, pick up and knit between the selvage sts along
the outside edge, picking up 2 sts for every 3 rows along straight edges,
3 sts for every 4 rows along slanted edges, and knitting each cast-on st.
Knit 1 row. Knit 10 more rows, increasing one st at each end every RS
row. Bind off loosely.

With RS facing and CC, pick up and knit along inside edge as for outside edge, knitting sts from back neck holder, and placing marker
before and after back neck sts. Knit 1 row. Knit 10 more rows, joining to
outside border at each end of every RS row by picking up and knitting a
st from outside border and working k2tog before first neck marker and
after second neck marker on each RS row.

**Note** If you plan to fasten the ends in back with buttons, on 4th RS row,
do not join edges, so that buttonhole will be created.

## SCALLOP EDGING

With RS facing, join CC at end of outside edge. With crochet hook, ch 1,
*(sc, ch 3, 3 dc) in same st, skip 4 sts; repeat from * to opposite end of
outside edge. Fasten off.
Work scallop edging along inside edge as for outside edge.

## FINISHING

Weave in ends and block lightly. If you plan to button ends in back, try
on shawl, crossing ends at chest and pulling to back. Mark position
where each tip hits lower back and attach button on tip at that point.
If not using buttons, sew ribbon, cord, tassels, or tie of choice onto each
end. Cut to desired length.

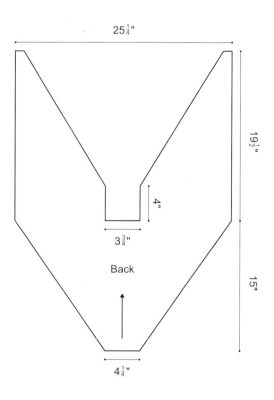

CHART

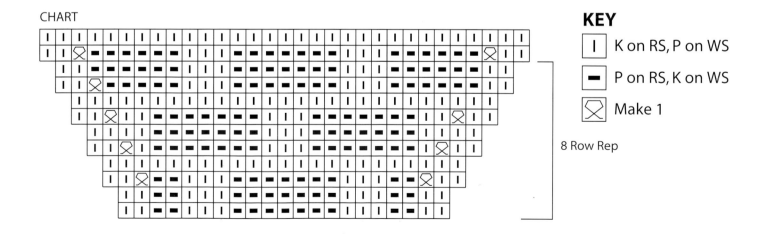

**KEY**

| I | K on RS, P on WS |
| — | P on RS, K on WS |
| ⊠ | Make 1 |

8 Row Rep

# The Catalina Stole

From the 1920s to the 1950s, swing dancers would cruise over to Catalina to dance at the casino. This stole would have been as useful on the boat as it was lovely on the dance floor. Worked today in cool, casual Microspun, this lovely length of lace seems better suited to an evening stroll on the beach or dinner by the bay. Of course, that doesn't mean you *couldn't* wear it dancing.

## CROCHET **EASY +**

### SIZE
21" x 74" (53.5 x 188 cm)

### MATERIALS
**(3)** LION BRAND Microspun
*2¹/₂ oz (70 g) 168 yd (154 m) Ball*
*100% Microfiber Acrylic*
- 6 balls #098 French Vanilla
  or color of your choice
- Size K-10.5 (6.5 mm) crochet hook
  OR SIZE TO OBTAIN GAUGE

### GAUGE
5 pattern repeats = 4³/₄" (12 cm).
BE SURE TO CHECK YOUR GAUGE.

### NOTE
Take care to maintain uniform loop sizes.

### STITCH EXPLANATION

**MK (Make Knot)**
Chain, pulling up ³/₄" (2 cm) loop; yarn over and draw through long loop; insert hook into stitch just made and single crochet.

### STOLE
Ch 64.

**Row 1** Dc in 4th ch from hook, sc in same ch, *MK, skip 2 ch, dc and sc in next ch; repeat from * across; turn—20 MK.

**Row 2** Ch 3, dc and sc in first sc, *MK, dc and sc in next sc; repeat from * across; turn.

Repeat Row 2 until stole measures 72" (183 cm) or desired length. Fasten off.

### LOOPED BORDER

**Row 1** Join yarn at any corner, ch 1, sc, *MK making a 1" (2.5 cm) loop, sc in center of t-ch or hole formed by MK; repeat from * around. Join with sc to beg sc; turn.

Repeat Row 1 two more times. Fasten off. Weave in ends. Block lightly, opening up lacework.

# Third-Time's-a-Charm Shawl

A precursor to today's popular poncho, this three-pointed shawl provides just the right amount of coverage for a chilly autumn day. You can work it up quickly in a trio of soft colors; fun fringe adds a playful note. Pretty, practical, and a pleasure to crochet—what more could you want?

## CROCHET **EASY**

### SIZE

**Length, excluding fringe** 30" (76 cm) back neck to back point

### MATERIALS

LION BRAND Wool-Ease
*3 oz (85 g) 197 yd (180 m) Ball*
*80% Acrylic, 20% Wool*
- 4 balls #104 Blush Heather (MC)
- 2 balls #139 Dark Rose Heather (A)
- 1 ball #140 Rose Heather (B)
  or colors of your choice
- Size P-15 (10 mm) crochet hook OR SIZE TO OBTAIN GAUGE
- Size K-10.5 (6.5 mm) crochet hook OR SIZE TO OBTAIN GAUGE

### GAUGE

9 hdc + 8 rows = 4" (10 cm) on larger hook.
8 Clusters + 8 rows = 4" (10 cm) on smaller hook.
BE SURE TO CHECK YOUR GAUGE.

**NOTE** Shawl begins at back neck and is worked down.

### STITCH EXPLANATION

#### CLUSTER

Yarn over, insert hook in next stitch, yarn over and draw up a loop, yarn over, draw through 2 loops on hook, yarn over, insert hook in same stitch, yarn over and draw up a loop, yarn over, draw through all 4 loops on hook.

### SHAWL

With MC and larger hook, ch 21.
**Row 1** Hdc in 3rd ch from hook and in each ch across; turn—20 hdc. Place marker between sts 10 and 11.
**Row 2** Ch 2, hdc in first st (one st increased), hdc in each st to one st before marker, work 2 hdc in each of the next 2 sts (2 sts increased), hdc in each st to last st, work 2 hdc in last st (one st increased); turn.
Repeat Row 2, increasing 4 sts per row (1 each edge and 2 center) until piece measures 22" (56 cm) from back neck to back point, or 8" (20.5 cm) less than desired length. Fasten off.

### BORDER

**Row 1** With A and smaller hook, ch 3, work 2 Clusters in first st (one stitch increased), work Cluster in each st to one st before center marker, work 2 Clusters in each of next 2 sts, (2 sts increased), work Cluster in each st to last st, work 2 Clusters in last st (one st increased); turn.
Repeat Border Row 1 for 12 more rows as follows: 1 row B, 1 row A, 6 rows B, 2 rows A, 2 rows MC. Fasten off.

## TOP EDGING

**Row 1** With smaller hook, join MC with slip stitch at side point. Ch 1, work 2 sc in first st, then work sc evenly spaced across top edge, ending 2 sc in last st; turn. Fasten off.

**Rows 2 and 3** With A, ch 1, work 2 sc in first st, sc in each sc to last st, work 2 sc in last st; turn. Fasten off.

## FRINGE

**For each fringe,** cut 4 strands of MC 8" (20.5 cm) long or desired length. Fold strands in half and, with crochet hook, pull fold through space between clusters around lower edge, forming a loop. Pull ends of fringe through this loop. Pull to tighten.

# The Perfect Shawl

Dark, dramatic, and ever-so-versatile, this quick-to-crochet cover-up will lend an air of mystery to anyone who wraps herself in it. Practical yet striking, it adds a bit of texture and drama to simple classics, from that little black dress to your favorite blue jeans.

CROCHET **EASY**

### SIZE

22" x 72" (56 x 183 cm), excluding fringe

### MATERIALS

**5** LION BRAND Homespun
*6 oz (170 g) 185 yd (169 m) Skein*
*98% Acrylic, 2% Polyester*

- 5 skeins #312 Edwardian or color of your choice
- Size N-13 (9 mm) crochet hook OR SIZE TO OBTAIN GAUGE
- Size K-10.5 (6.5 mm) crochet hook

### GAUGE

1 pattern repeat = 4" (10 cm) on larger hook.

BE SURE TO CHECK YOUR GAUGE.

### STOLE

With larger hook, ch 50.

**Row 1** Sc in 2nd ch from hook and in each ch across; turn—49 sc.

**Row 2** Ch 3, dc in next 3 sc, *skip 2 sc, 4 dc in next sc (*Shell made*), skip 2 sc, dc in next 4 sc; repeat from * across; turn—5 Shells.

**Row 3** Ch 3, front post dc (see Techniques, page 188) in next 3 dc, *skip 2 dc, 4 dc between 2nd and 3rd dc of Shell, front post dc in next 4 dc; repeat from * across; turn.

Repeat Row 3 until stole measures 72" (183 cm) or desired length. Fasten off, or continue with Looped Fringe.

### LOOPED FRINGE (OPTIONAL)

With smaller hook, ch 1, sc in first st, ch 18, sc in same st, *ch 18, sc in next st; repeat from * across. Fasten off. Repeat along opposite end of stole. Weave in ends.

# The Pamela Stole

We're not sure who Pamela was, but we are certain she had a great sense of style. How do we know? Just take one look at the lacy, lovely wrap that bears her name. Pamela liked fuzzy mohair, but we've substituted a sleek and striking ribbon yarn for a more modern, yet equally luxurious, look. We're sure Pamela would approve.

## KNIT **EASY**

### SIZE

20" x 66" (51 x 167.5 cm), excluding
fringe

### MATERIALS

**6** LION BRAND Incredible
1³/₄ oz (50 g) 110 yd (100 m) Ball
100% Nylon

- 7 balls #203 City Lights
  or color of your choice
- Size 13 (9 mm) knitting needles
  or SIZE TO OBTAIN GAUGE
- Size N-13 (9 mm) crochet hook

### GAUGE

9 sts + 16 rows = 4" (10 cm) in Pattern stitch.
BE SURE TO CHECK YOUR GAUGE.

### STOLE

Cast on 46 sts. Knit 3 rows for border.
**Next Row** Knit 2, *knit 1, yarn over, knit 2 together; repeat from * to last 2 stitches, knit 2.
Repeat this row until piece measures 65" (165 cm), or 1" (2.5 cm) less than desired length. Knit 3 rows. Bind off loosely.

### FRINGE

For each fringe, cut 3 strands of yarn 20" (51 cm) long or desired length. Fold strands in half and, with crochet hook, pull folded strands through Stole, forming a loop. Pull ends of fringe through this loop. Pull to tighten. Attach fringe along each end of Stole. Trim fringe evenly.

# Putting on the Glitz

Accomplished with an easy-to-crochet rectangle of knot stitches, this simple scarf showed plenty of potential. Light, lacy, and designed to drape, it was a little too demure for our tastes. We decided to rev it up with vibrant color and a bit of sparkle, courtesy of a glittery metallic yarn. How divine.

## CROCHET **EASY**

### SIZE

9″ x 60″ (23 x 152.5 cm), excluding
    fringe

### MATERIALS

**4** LION BRAND Glitterspun
*1³/₄ oz (50 g) 115 yd (105 m) Ball*
*60 % Acrylic, 27% Cupro, 13% Polyester*
- 3 balls #113 Ruby
  or color of your choice
- Size K-10.5 (6.5 mm) crochet hook
  OR SIZE TO OBTAIN GAUGE

### GAUGE

4 Knot pattern repeats = 4″ (10 cm).
BE SURE TO CHECK YOUR GAUGE.

### NOTE Take care to maintain
uniform loop sizes.

### STITCH EXPLANATIONS

**MAIN KNOT**

Chain 1, pulling up a ³/₄″ (2 cm) loop; yarn over and draw through long loop; insert hook in stitch before long loop and single crochet.

**EDGE KNOT**

Chain 1, pulling up a ¹/₂″ (1.5 cm) loop; yarn over and draw through long loop; insert hook in stitch before long loop and single crochet.

### SCARF

**Foundation Row** Ch 2, sc in 2nd ch from hook, work 18 Edge Knots, end with 1 Main Knot; turn.

**Row 1** Work 1 sc in sc between 3rd and 4th loops from hook, *work 2 Main Knots, skip 2 loops, sc in next sc; repeat from * across; turn.

**Row 2** Work 2 Edge Knots, work 1 Main Knot, sc in sc between 4th and 5th loops from hook, *work 2 Main Knots, skip 2 loops, sc in next sc; repeat from * across, ending in top of Edge Knot; turn.

Repeat Row 2 until Scarf measures 60″ (152.5 cm) or desired length.

**Last Row** Work 2 Edge Knots, sc in sc between 3rd and 4th loops from hook, *work 2 Edge Knots, skip 2 loops, sc in next sc; repeat from * across. Fasten off.

### FRINGE

Join yarn with slip stitch at corner of Scarf. *Ch 30, slip stitch in next st; repeat from * 17 more times across short edge of Scarf. Fasten off. Repeat along other short edge.

### FINISHING

Block lightly, opening up lacework.

# CHAPTER 4

# A Family Affair: Sweaters for Everyone

There was a time when any homemaker worth her salt would keep her family clothed in warm sweaters, toasty mittens, and wool socks. That skill with yarn and needles may have skipped a generation or two, but if today's surge in the number of knitters and crocheters is any indication, today's women (and men) are once again generously bestowing the fruits of their labor on family and friends.

Anyone who has been on the giving or receiving end of a handmade gift knows there's nothing like it. A sweater created by loving hands is a one-of-a-kind expression of affection that you just can't buy ready-made.

# The Go-Everywhere Cardigan

Paired with knickers and knee socks, double-breasted cardigans like this were once the mainstay of every well-dressed child's wardrobe. Today's kid is more likely to toss it on over a tee shirt and jeans. With that in mind, we chose to offer it in a rough-and-tumble, machine-washable yarn that will look good for years to come.

KNIT with CROCHET edging **EASY +**

## SIZES

Child's 2 (4, 6, 8, 10)

**Finished chest** 28 (30½, 32½, 36, 38)" [71 (77.5, 82.5, 91.5, 96.5) cm]

**Length** 13 (14, 15, 16, 17)" [33 (35.5, 38, 40.5, 43) cm]

**Note** Before beginning pattern, circle all numbers pertaining to your size for ease in working.

## MATERIALS

(4) LION BRAND Wool-Ease

*3 oz (85 g) 197 yd (180 m) Ball*

*80% Acrylic, 20% Wool*

- 4 (4, 5, 5, 6) balls #138 Cranberry or color of your choice
- Size 9 (5.5 mm) knitting needles OR SIZE TO OBTAIN GAUGE
- Size 7 (4.5 mm) knitting needles
- Size H-8 (5 mm) crochet hook
- Six ⅞" (22 mm) buttons
- Large-eyed, blunt needle

## GAUGE

16 sts + 38 rows = 4" (10 cm) in Brioche Stitch with larger needles.

BE SURE TO CHECK YOUR GAUGE.

## PATTERN STITCH

### BRIOCHE STITCH (Multiple of 2 sts)

**Note** The yarn is brought to the front between the needles before each slipped stitch. When working the next k or k2tog, the yarn is brought over the needle (not between the needles) to the back in order to work the stitch. Work all slipped stitches as if to purl.

**Row 1** *K 1, yarn forward, slip 1; repeat from *.

**Row 2** K 1, yarn forward, slip 1, *k2tog, yarn forward, slip 1; repeat from *.

Repeat Row 2 for Brioche Stitch.

## BACK

With larger needles, cast on 52 (58, 62, 68, 72) sts. Work in Brioche Stitch for 13 (14, 15, 16, 17)" [33 (35.5, 38, 40.5, 43) cm]. Bind off loosely.

## LEFT FRONT

With larger needles, cast on 36 (38, 40, 44, 46) sts. Work in Brioche Stitch for 7 (8, 9, 9¼, 10¼)" [18 (20.5, 23, 23.5, 26) cm]. Dec one st at neck edge every 3rd row 19 (19, 19, 21, 21) times—17 (19, 21, 23, 25) sts remain. Work even until piece measures same as Back. Bind off.

## RIGHT FRONT

Work as for Left Front, reversing shaping.

## SLEEVES

With larger needles, cast on 40 (44, 48, 52, 56) sts. Work in Brioche Stitch for 7 (9, 10, 11, 12)" [18 (23, 25.5, 28, 30.5) cm] or desired Sleeve length, ending with a WS row.

**Cuff** Change to smaller needles.

**Next row (RS)** *K 1, k2tog, p 1; repeat from * to last 4 sts, k 1, k2tog, k 1—30 (33, 36, 39, 42) sts remain.

**Next row** P 3, *k 1, p 2; repeat from *.

Continue in K 2, P 1 Rib as established until Cuff measures 4¹/₂" (11.5 cm). Bind off in rib.

## FINISHING

Sew shoulder seams. Sew on Sleeves. Sew side and Sleeve seams. Sew buttons evenly spaced between neck shaping and bottom edge, 3 on each side, about 3" (7.5 cm) from edge (see photo).

**Edging and buttonholes**

Mark positions for button loops on Right Front for girls, Left Front for boys.

**Row 1** With RS facing and crochet hook, work sc up Right Front edge, around Back neck, and down Left Front edge. DO NOT TURN.

**Row 2** Ch 1, work reverse single crochet (see Techniques, page 188) along Fronts and Back neck and, AT THE SAME TIME, ch 3 and skip one st at button loop positions. Fasten off. Weave in ends.

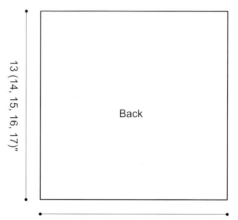

13 (14, 15, 16, 17)"

Back

13 (14½, 15½, 17, 18)"

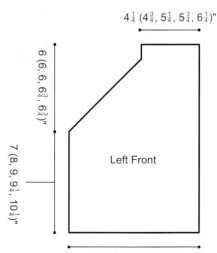

4¼ (4¾, 5¼, 5¾, 6¼)"

6 (6, 6, 6¾, 6¾)"

7 (8, 9, 9¼, 10¼)"

Left Front

9 (9½, 10, 11, 11½)"

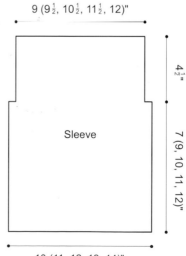

9 (9½, 10½, 11½, 12)"

4½"

7 (9, 10, 11, 12)"

Sleeve

10 (11, 12, 13, 14)"

A Family Affair: Sweaters for Everyone 83

# The Sailor Sweater

Shirley Temple meets the French Riviera in this utterly adorable, updated interpretation of the child's middy. We wanted this to appeal to the tomboys out there, too, so we replaced the original wide ribbon ties with sportier crisscross lacing.

## KNIT **EASY**

### SIZE

Child's 2 (4, 6, 8, 10)

**Finished chest** 26 1/2 (28, 30, 32, 34)" [67.5 (71, 76, 81.5, 86.5) cm]

**Length** 15 3/4 (17 1/2, 20 1/2, 23, 25)" [40 (44.5, 52, 58.5, 63.5) cm]

**Note** Before beginning pattern, circle all numbers pertaining to your size for ease in working.

### MATERIALS

(4) LION BRAND Cotton-Ease
3 1/2 oz (100 g) 207 yd (188 m) Ball
50% Cotton, 50% Acrylic

- 3 (3, 4, 5, 6) balls #109 Blueberry (MC)
- 1 ball #100 Vanilla (CC) or colors of your choice
- Size 8 (5 mm) 24" (60 cm) circular needle OR SIZE TO OBTAIN GAUGE
- Large-eyed, blunt needle

### GAUGE

17 sts + 34 rows = 4" (10 cm) in Garter stitch (knit every row).
BE SURE TO CHECK YOUR GAUGE.

**NOTE** This garment is worked in one piece starting at the bottom Back, casting on stitches for the Sleeves, working over the shoulders and down the Front.

## BODY

With CC, cast on 56 (60, 64, 68, 72) sts using long tail cast on (see Techniques, page 189). K 16 rows. Change to MC and k every row until piece measures 9 3/4 (11, 13 1/2, 15 1/2, 17)" [25 (28, 34.5, 39.5, 43) cm] from beg of MC, ending with a RS row.

**Begin sleeves** Cast on 30 (34, 38, 45, 57) sts at the end of next 2 rows using cable cast on method (see Techniques, p. 189 )—116 (128, 140, 158, 186) sts. Knit every row until piece measures 4 (4 1/2, 5, 5 1/2, 6)" [10 (11.5, 12.5, 14, 15) cm] from beg of Sleeve, ending with a WS row.

**Divide for back neck** K 48 (53, 58, 67, 81) sts, join 2nd ball of yarn and bind off center 20 (22, 24, 24, 24) sts, knit to end. Working both sides at same time, k 10 (12, 14, 16, 18) rows, then cast on 10 (11, 12, 12, 12) sts at each neck edge—116 (128, 140, 158, 186) sts. Work each side even until Sleeve measures 8 (9, 10, 11, 12)" [20.5 (23, 25.5, 28, 30.5) cm], ending with a WS row.

**Join Fronts and Sleeves** Bind off 30 (34, 38, 45, 57) sts at beg of row, knit to end of Right Front. With same ball of yarn, knit across Left Front to join pieces. Bind off 30 (34, 38, 45, 57) sts at beg of next row—56 (60, 64, 68, 72) sts remain. Work even until Front measures 9 3/4 (11, 13 1/2, 15 1/2, 17)" [25 (28, 34.5, 39.5, 43) cm] from end of Sleeve, ending with a WS row. Change to CC and knit 16 rows. Bind off all sts.

## COLLAR

With WS facing and CC, beginning at Front neck cast-on, pick up and knit 40 (45, 50, 52, 54) sts around neck. (Do not pick up sts in slit.) Knit every row for 3 (3 1/2, 3 1/2, 4, 4)" [7.5 (9, 9, 10, 10) cm] or desired Collar length. Bind off.

## CUFFS

With CC, pick up and k 34 (38, 42, 47, 51) sts along bottom edge of Sleeve. K 32 rows. Bind off very loosely.

## FINISHING

Sew side seams, beginning at MC portion of body, leaving CC edges open. Sew Sleeve seams, folding back Cuff. Weave in ends.

## TIE

With CC, cast on 3 sts and work I-cord (see Techniques, page 188) for about 30" (76 cm). Fasten off. Lace up Front opening for about 3" (7.5 cm), as in picture, pulling cord through spaces between stitches, then tie in bow.

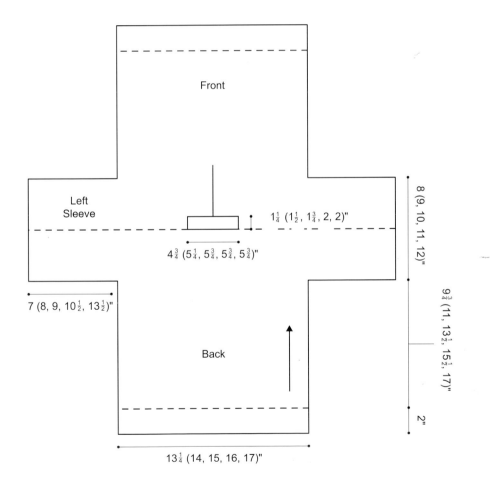

Front

Left Sleeve

$1\frac{1}{4}$ ($1\frac{1}{2}$, $1\frac{3}{4}$, 2, 2)"

$4\frac{3}{4}$ ($5\frac{1}{4}$, $5\frac{3}{4}$, $5\frac{3}{4}$, $5\frac{3}{4}$)"

8 (9, 10, 11, 12)"

$9\frac{3}{4}$ (11, $13\frac{1}{2}$, $15\frac{1}{2}$, 17)"

2"

7 (8, 9, $10\frac{1}{2}$, $13\frac{1}{2}$)"

Back

$13\frac{1}{4}$ (14, 15, 16, 17)"

# The Textured Turtleneck

Rugged and ready for anything, this classic ribbed pullover is perfect for playtime. The modern yarn and extra ease make a softer and more comfortable sweater to wear than the original. Today's moms will appreciate its hard-wearing and easy-care qualities.

KNIT **EASY +**

## SIZE

Child's 4 (6, 8, 10)

**Finished chest** 26 1/2 (29 1/2, 32 1/2, 35)" [67.5 (75, 82.5, 89) cm]

**Length** 14 1/2 (16, 18 1/2, 21 1/2)" [37 (40.5, 47, 54.5) cm]

**Note** Before beginning pattern, circle all numbers pertaining to your size for ease in working.

## MATERIALS

**5** LION BRAND Wool-Ease Chunky
5 oz (140 g) 153 yd (140 m) Ball
80% Acrylic, 20% Wool

- 4 (5, 7, 9) balls #107 Bluebell or color of your choice
- Size 10.5 (6.5 mm) knitting needles OR SIZE TO OBTAIN GAUGE
- Size 8 (5 mm) knitting needles
- Size 8 (5 mm) 16" (40 cm) circular needle
- Stitch holders
- Large-eyed, blunt needle

## GAUGE

17 sts + 20 rows = 4" (10 cm) in 1 x 1 Garter Rib on larger needles.
BE SURE TO CHECK YOUR GAUGE.

**NOTE** Maintain first and last stitch in Stockinette stitch (knit on RS, purl on WS) for selvage on Back and Front. Maintain first and last 2 stitches in Stockinette stitch for selvage on Sleeves.

## PATTERN STITCH

GARTER RIB  **(Multiple of 6 sts + 5)**

**Row 1** (RS) K 1 (edge st), *k 1, p 1, k 1, p 3; repeat from * to last 4 sts, k 1, p 1, k 2.

**Row 2** P 1 (edge st), p 1, *k 1, p 1; repeat from * to last st, p 1 (edge st).

## BACK

With smaller needles, cast on 59 (65, 71, 77) sts using long tail cast on. Work 2 rows in Reverse Stockinette Stitch (p on RS, k on WS). Change to larger needles. Work even in Garter Rib until piece measures 8 (9, 11, 13)" [20.5 (23, 28, 33) cm] from beg, ending with a WS row.

**Shape armholes** Bind off 3 sts at beg of next 2 rows—53 (59, 65, 71) sts remain. Maintaining selvage st, work even until armhole measures 6 1/2 (7, 7 1/2, 8 1/2)" [16.5 (18, 19, 21.5) cm]. Place sts on holder.

## FRONT

Work as for Back until armhole measures 2 (2 1/2, 2 1/2, 3)" [5 (6.5, 6.5, 7.5) cm], ending with a WS row.

**Shape neck** Work 20 (22, 25, 27) sts, put center 13 (15, 15, 17) sts on holder, work to end. Working both sides at same time, dec one st at neck edge every other row 3 (3, 4, 4) times—17 (19, 21, 23) sts remain each side. Work even until Front measures same as Back. Place remaining sts on holders for shoulders.

## SLEEVES

With smaller needles, cast on 29 (31, 33, 35) sts using long-tail cast-on (see Techniques, page 188). Work 2 rows in Reverse Stockinette Stitch.

**Next row (RS)** K 2, *p 1, k 1; repeat from * to last st, k 1.

**Next row** P 2, *k 1, p 1; repeat from * to last st, p 1.

Repeat these 2 rows until Sleeve measures 2" (5 cm), ending with a WS row. Change to larger needles.

**Set-up row (RS)** K 2 (edge sts); p 0 (0, 0, 1), k 0 (0, 1, 1), p 2 (3, 3, 3); work 3 repeats [6 sts each] of 1 x 1 Garter Rib, k 1, p 1, k 1; p 2 (3, 3, 3), k 0 (0, 1, 1), p 0 (0, 0, 1); k 2 (edge sts).

Work 3 rows in pattern as established.

**Inc Row** K 2, M1L (see Techniques, page 188), work in pattern to last 2 sts, M1R (see Techniques, page 188), k 2.

Work Inc Row every other row 3 (3, 2, 5) more times, then every 4th row 10 (11, 13, 13) times, working incs into pattern—57 (61, 65, 73) sts.

Work even until Sleeve measures 13 (14, 15, 16)" [33 (35.5, 38, 40.5) cm] from beg. Bind off in pattern.

### FINISHING

Place sts from Front and Back on needles and, with right sides facing, seam shoulders with 3-Needle Bind Off (see Techniques, page 188) across 17 (19, 21, 23) shoulder sts, bind off 19 (21, 23, 25) Back neck sts, 3-Needle Bind Off across remaining shoulder sts.

**Turtleneck**

With RS facing and circular needle, pick up and knit 48 (54, 58, 64) sts evenly spaced around neck. Work in K 1, P 1 Rib for 2" (5 cm) or desired length. P 2 rows. Bind off very loosely in purl.

Sew in Sleeves. Sew side and Sleeve seams. Weave in ends.

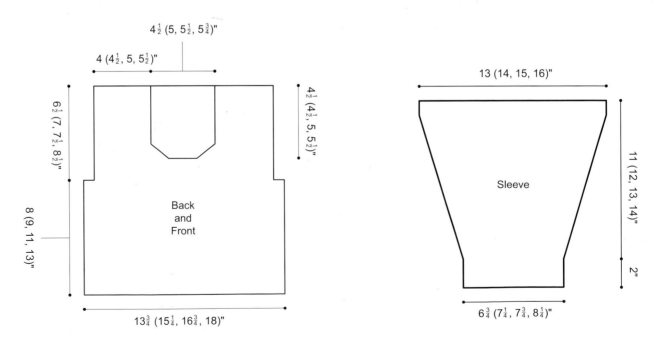

4½ (5, 5½, 5¾)"

4 (4½, 5, 5½)"

6½ (7, 7½, 8½)"

4½ (4½, 5, 5½)"

8 (9, 11, 13)"

Back and Front

13¾ (15¼, 16¾, 18)"

13 (14, 15, 16)"

Sleeve

11 (12, 13, 14)"

2"

6¾ (7¼, 7¾, 8¼)"

# The Striped Raglan

From pushing a stroller through the park on a fine autumn afternoon to sipping a hot toddy après ski, you will find that this timeless sweater has the kind of easygoing yet still pulled-together look that's perfect for any occasion. We've substituted a lightweight textured yarn in a soothing palette of green and gray for the original mohair.

## KNIT INTERMEDIATE

### SIZES

S (M, L, 1X, 2X)

**Finished chest** 40 (44, 48, 52, 56)" [101.5 (112, 122, 132, 142) cm]

**Length** 24 1/2 (25, 25, 25 3/4, 26 3/4)" [62 (63.5, 63.5, 65.5, 68) cm]

**Note** Before beginning pattern, circle all numbers pertaining to your size.

### MATERIALS

**6** LION BRAND Watercolors

*1 3/4 oz (50 g) 55 yd (50 m) Ball*

*65% Acrylic, 35% Merino Wool*

- 3 balls #398 Bright Clouds (A)
- 6 balls #352 Mist Grey (B)
- 4 balls #373 Pond Green (C) or colors of your choice
- Sizes 10 (6 mm) and 11 (8 mm) 29" (70 cm) circular needles OR SIZE TO OBTAIN GAUGE
- Sizes 10 (6 mm) and 11 (8 mm) 16" (40 cm) circular needles
- Sizes 10 (6 mm) and 11 (8 mm) double-pointed needles
- Stitch holders
- Stitch markers
- Large-eyed, blunt needle

### GAUGE

10 sts + 16 rnds = 4" (10 cm) in Pattern Stitch on larger needles.

BE SURE TO CHECK YOUR GAUGE.

**NOTE** Body and Sleeves are worked separately in the round to the underarms, then joined together for the raglan yoke and knit to the neck.

### PATTERN STITCH

**Round 1** Knit.

**Round 2** *K 1, p 1; repeat from *.

Repeat Rounds 1 and 2 for pattern.

### STRIPE SEQUENCE

*2 rounds A, 14 rounds B, 2 rounds A, 10 rounds C; repeat from * for Stripe Sequence.

### BODY

With smaller 29" (70 cm) circular needle and A, cast on 100 (110, 120, 130, 140) sts. Join, being careful not to twist, and place marker to indicate beg of round. Work in K1, P1 Rib for 2" (5 cm). Change to larger needle and Pattern Stitch and, AT THE SAME TIME, begin Stripe Sequence. Work even until piece measures 14 1/2 (14 1/2, 14 1/2, 15, 15 1/2)" [37 (37, 37, 38, 39.5) cm] from beginning. Leave piece on needle and set aside.

### SLEEVES

With smaller double-pointed needles and A, cast on 20 (22, 24, 26, 28) sts. Join, being careful not to twist, and place marker. Work in K1, P1 Rib for 2 1/2" (6.5 cm). Change to larger doubled-pointed needles and Pattern Stitch and begin Stripe Sequence with 10 rounds C. After working 3rd round of C, begin inc.

**Round 4 (Inc Round)** K 1, knit into front and back of next stitch, work to last st, knit into front and back of last st.

Repeat Inc Round every 5th round 0 (0, 3, 10, 11) times; every 6th round 2 (8, 6, 0, 0) times; and every 7th round 5 (0, 0, 0, 0) times, working all increases into pattern and changing to circular needle when possible—36 (40, 44, 48, 52) sts. Work even until piece measures 17½ (17½, 17½, 18, 18½)" [44.5 (44.5, 44.5, 45.5, 47) cm] from beg, ending at same point in Stripe Sequence as on Body. On last round, end 3 (4, 5, 5, 6) sts before marker. Slip next 7 (9, 11, 11, 13) sts to holder. Place remaining sts onto separate stitch holder.

## JOIN FOR RAGLAN YOKE

Work 43 (47, 49, 53, 57) Body sts, place marker, place next 7 (8, 11, 12, 13) sts on holder, work 29 (31, 33, 37, 39) Sleeve sts, place marker, work 43 (47, 49, 53, 57) Body sts, place remaining 7 (8, 11, 12, 13) sts on holder, place marker, work 29 (31, 33, 37, 39) sts of 2nd Sleeve, place marker and join—144 (156, 164, 180, 192) sts. Maintain Stripe Sequence through yoke.

**Next 4 rounds** *K 1, work in pattern to one st before next marker, k 1, slip marker; repeat from *.

**Dec Round** *Ssk (see Techniques, page 188), work in pattern to 2 sts before next marker, k2tog, slip marker; repeat from *—8 sts decreased. Repeat Dec Round every 3rd round 9 (9, 9, 6, 6) times, then every other round 3 (4, 4, 9, 10) times, changing to shorter circular needle when needed—40 (44, 52, 52, 56) sts. Work 1 round even. Leave remaining sts on needle. Break yarn.

## FINISHING

Change to smaller 16" (40 cm) circular needle and A and work in K1, P1 Rib for 1" (2.5 cm). Bind off very loosely in rib.

Slip 7 (8, 11, 12, 13) underarm Body sts and 7 (9, 11, 11, 13) underarm Sleeve sts onto 2 needles. Using matching yarn and with RS tog, work 3-Needle Bind Off (see Techniques, page 188).

**Note** Size M and size 1X have 1 extra underarm Body stitch.

In middle of bind off row, bind off 2 Body sts with 1 Sleeve st.

Weave in ends.

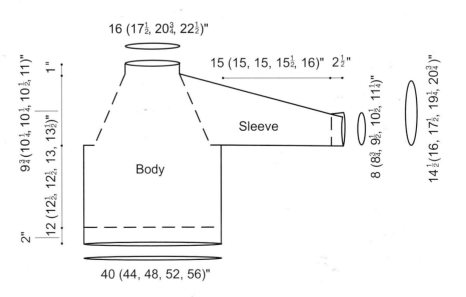

16 (17½, 20¾, 22½)"

15 (15, 15, 15½, 16)"  2½"

9¾ (10¼, 10¼, 10½, 11)"

1"

12 (12½, 12½, 13, 13½)"

2"

Body

Sleeve

8 (8¾, 9½, 10½, 11¼)"

14½ (16, 17½, 19¼, 20¾)"

40 (44, 48, 52, 56)"

# The Ski Sweater

Some sweaters—like some men—just get better with age. Take this classic pullover. Knit in an easy-care wool blend, it's still in its prime and looking good for either a gal or a guy.

## SIZES

S (M, L, 1X, 2X)

**Finished chest** 45 (48$\frac{1}{2}$, 53$\frac{1}{2}$, 57$\frac{1}{2}$, 61$\frac{1}{2}$)" [114.5 (123, 136, 146, 156) cm]

**Length** 25 (26$\frac{1}{4}$, 28, 30$\frac{1}{4}$, 30$\frac{3}{4}$)" [63.5 (66.5, 71, 77, 78) cm]

**Note** Before beginning pattern, circle all numbers pertaining to your size for ease in working.

## MATERIALS

**⑤** LION BRAND Wool-Ease Chunky
*80% Acrylic, 20% Wool*
*5 oz (140 g) 153 yd (140 m) Ball*

- 6 (7, 7, 8, 9) balls #178 Nantucket or color of your choice
- Size 10.5 (6.5 mm) knitting needles OR SIZE TO OBTAIN GAUGE
- Size 9 (5.5 mm) knitting needles
- Size 9 (5.5 mm) 16" (40 cm) circular needle
- Large-eyed, blunt needle

## GAUGE

12.5 sts + 20 rows = 4" (10 cm) in Pattern Stitch on larger needles.
BE SURE TO CHECK YOUR GAUGE.

**NOTE** Row gauge is important when working a raglan sweater.

## PATTERN STITCH

**Row 1 (RS)** K 1, *k 1, p 1; repeat from * to last st, k 1.

**Row 2** Purl.

Repeat Rows 1 and 2 for Pattern Stitch.

All increases and decreases are worked 2 stitches from edge as follows:

**Dec row (RS)** K 2, ssk (see Techniques, page 188), work to last 4 sts, k2tog, k 2.

**Dec row (WS)** P 2, p2tog, work to last 4 sts, ssp (see Techniques, page 188), p 2.

**Inc row** Work 2 sts, M1R (see Techniques, page 188), work to last 2 sts, M1L (see Techniques, page 188), work 2 sts.

## BACK

With smaller needles, cast on 70 (76, 84, 90, 96) sts.

**Row 1 (RS)** K 1, *k 1, p 1; repeat from * to last st, k 1.

**Row 2** P 1, *k 1, p 1; repeat from * to last st, p 1.

Repeat these 2 rows until ribbing measures 2$\frac{1}{2}$" (6.5 cm), ending with a WS row.

Change to larger needles, begin Pattern Stitch and work even until piece measures 15 (15$\frac{1}{2}$, 16, 17, 17$\frac{1}{4}$)" [38 (39.5, 40.5, 43, 44) cm] from beg, or desired length to underarm, ending with a WS row.

**Shape raglan** Bind off 6 (6, 6, 7, 8) sts at beg of next 2 rows. Dec one st each end every 3rd row 8 (8, 10, 12, 16) times, then every other row 12 (14, 14, 14, 9) times—18 (20, 24, 24, 30) sts remain. Bind off.

## FRONT

Work as for Back until armhole measures 7 (7$\frac{1}{2}$, 8, 9, 9$\frac{1}{2}$)" [18 (19, 20.5, 23, 24) cm], ending with a WS row.

**Shape Front neck** Continue with raglan shaping and, AT THE SAME TIME, work to center 12 (12, 14, 14, 18) sts. Attach 2nd ball of yarn and bind off center 12 (12, 14, 14, 18) sts, work to end. Working both sides

at the same time, dec one st each neck edge every RS row 3 (4, 5, 5, 6) times. When raglan shaping is complete, fasten off.

### SLEEVES

With smaller needles, cast on 32 (32, 36, 40, 42) sts. Work ribbing as for Back. Change to larger needles, begin Pattern Stitch and inc one st each end every 5th row 0 (6, 0, 4, 0) times; every 6th row 10 (8, 14, 11, 6) times; and every 7th row 2 (0, 0, 0, 8) times, working all incs into pattern—56 (60, 64, 70, 70) sts. Work even until piece measures 18 (19, 20, 20$^1$/$_2$, 21$^1$/$_2$)" [45.5 (48.5, 52, 54.5) cm] from beg, ending with a WS row. **Shape raglan** Bind off 6 (6, 6, 7, 8) sts at beg of next 2 rows. Dec one st each end every 3rd row 8 (8, 10, 12, 16) times, then every other row 12 (14, 14, 14, 9) times. Bind off remaining 4 sts.

### FINISHING

Sew raglan, side, and Sleeve seams.
**Neckband** With circular needle, pick up and knit 68 (70, 76, 80, 94) sts around neck. Work in K1, P1 Rib for 1" (2.5 cm). Bind off very loosely in pattern. Weave in ends.

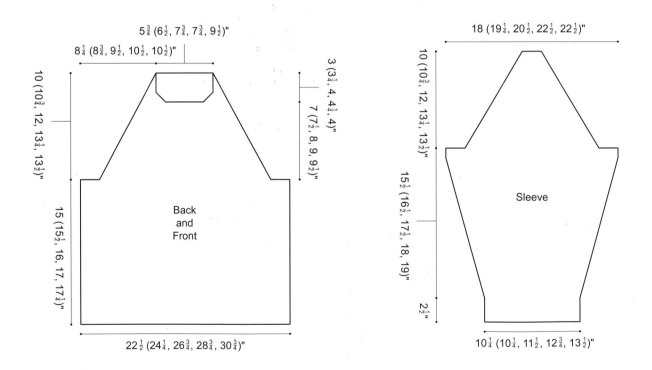

# The Best-Friend Sweater

Unconditional love and a willingness to listen to your every woe without passing judgment makes your pooch worth pampering. Knit in machine washable wool, this doggone handsome sweater ensures that come winter, Rover's body will stay as warm as his heart.

KNIT **EASY +**

## SIZE

S (M, L, XL)

**Chest circumference** 16 1/2 (23 1/2, 30 3/4, 36 3/4)" [42 (59.5, 78, 93.5) cm]

**Neck circumference** 10 (14, 18, 21 1/4) [25.5 (35.5, 45.5, 54) cm]

**Note** Sizes are based approximately on the measurements of a Maltese, a Cocker Spaniel, a Boxer, and a Labrador Retriever. Before beginning, circle all numbers pertaining to your size.

## MATERIALS

**(4)** LION BRAND Wool-Ease

*3 oz (85 g) 197 yd (180 m) Ball*
*80% Acrylic, 20% Wool*

- 2 (3, 4, 5) balls #179 Chestnut Heather
  or color of your choice
- Size 7 (4.5 mm) knitting needles
- Size 8 (5 mm) knitting needles
  OR SIZE TO OBTAIN GAUGE
- Size 6 (4 mm) double-pointed needles
- Stitch holders
- One 7/8" (22 mm) snap (optional)
- Large-eyed, blunt needle

## GAUGE

20 sts + 30 rows = 4" (10 cm) in Block Pattern on largest needles.
BE SURE TO CHECK YOUR GAUGE.

**NOTE** Dog sweater begins at Neck ribbing.

## PATTERN STITCH

BLOCK PATTERN    **(Multiple of 16 sts + 16)**

**Rows 1-3** K 8, *p 3, k 3; repeat from * to last 8 sts, k 8.

**Rows 4-6** K 8, *k 3, p 3; repeat from * to last 8 sts, k 8.

Repeat Rows 1-6 for Block Pattern.

## SWEATER

With middle-sized needles, cast on 50 (70, 90, 106) sts.

**Row 1 (RS)** K 1, *k 2, p 2; repeat from * to last st, k 1.

**Row 2** P 1, *k 2, p 2; repeat from * to last st, p 1.

Continue in rib as established for 2 1/2 (3 1/2, 4 1/2, 5 1/2)" [6.5 (9, 11.5, 14) cm], ending with a WS row.

Change to largest needles.

**Next row** *K 3, M1 (see Techniques, page 188); repeat from * to last 2 (4, 3, 4) sts, k to end—66 (92, 119, 140) sts.

**Next row** Knit.

**Next row** *K 5, M1; repeat from * to last 1 (2, 4, 5) sts, knit to end—79 (110, 142, 167) sts.

**Next row** Knit.

**Next row** Knit, increasing 3 (8, 12, 17) sts evenly spaced across—82 (118, 154, 184) sts.

K 3 (5, 5, 5) rows.

Begin Block Pattern and work even until piece measures 5 (6, 7, 10)" [12.5 (15, 18, 25.5) cm] from end of ribbing, ending with a WS row.

**Leg openings** Maintaining pattern as established, work 8 (12, 17, 19) sts, place next 7 (10, 12, 15) sts on holder, attach 2nd ball of yarn and work to last 15 (22, 29, 34) sts, place 7 (10, 12, 15) sts on holder, attach 3rd ball of yarn and work to end.

Work 3 sections even for 1¹/₂ (2, 2¹/₂, 3)" [4 (5, 6.5, 7.5) cm], ending with a WS row.

**Joining row** Using only first ball of yarn, work to first opening, cast on 7 (10, 12, 15) sts, work to 2nd opening, cast on 7 (10, 12, 15) sts, work to end—82 (118, 154, 184) sts.

Continue in pattern as established for 1¹/₂ (3, 3, 3¹/₄)" 4 (7.5, 7.5, 8.5) cm] from end of leg openings, ending with a WS row.

**Dec Row** K 7, k2tog, work pattern as established to last 9 sts, ssk (see Techniques, page 188 ), knit to end.

**Next row** K 8, work pattern as established to last 8 sts, k 8.

Repeat these 2 rows 10 (16, 24, 26) more times—60 (84, 104, 130) sts remain. Work even until piece measures 12 (17, 20, 25)" [30.5 (43, 51, 63.5) cm] from end of ribbing (or 1¹/₄" [3 cm] less than desired length from neck to tail, before edging), ending with a WS row. K 12 rows. Bind off.

Sew chest seam from neck rib to beginning of decreases.

**Sleeves** With double-pointed needles, pick up and knit 32 (56, 60, 68) sts around leg openings, including sts on holders. Join and work in K 2, P 2 Rib for 1" (2.5 cm) or desired length. Bind off in rib.

**Edging (optional)** Work crochet Shell around back flap edge as follows: Join yarn with slip stitch at chest seam, ch 1, *sc in next st, skip 2 sts or ridges, work 5 dc in next st or ridge, skip 2 sts or ridges; repeat from * around; join with slip stitch to beg sc. Fasten off.

**Tail strap (optional)** Cast on 16 (20, 25, 30) sts. K 14 rows. Bind off. Sew one end of strap on back of sweater just left of center. Sew snap on other end of strap. Sew opposite side of snap to back of sweater, just right of center. Weave in ends.

# Stitch Pattern Chart for Dog Sweater

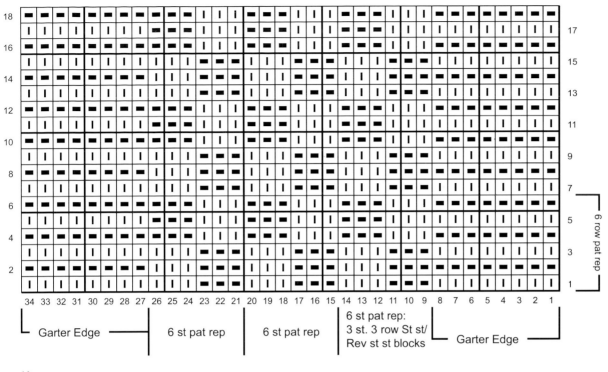

Garter Edge | 6 st pat rep | 6 st pat rep | 6 st pat rep: 3 st. 3 row St st/ Rev st st blocks | Garter Edge

6 row pat rep

Key

 K on RS, P on WS

■ P on RS, K on WS

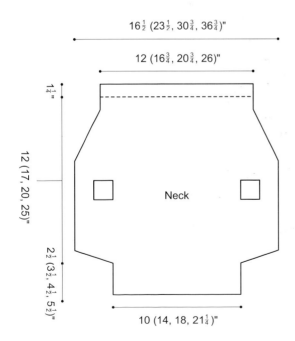

$16\frac{1}{2}$ ($23\frac{1}{2}$, $30\frac{3}{4}$, $36\frac{3}{4}$)"

12 ($16\frac{3}{4}$, $20\frac{3}{4}$, 26)"

$1\frac{1}{4}$"

12 (17, 20, 25)"

$2\frac{1}{2}$ ($3\frac{1}{2}$, $4\frac{1}{2}$, $5\frac{1}{2}$)"

Neck

10 (14, 18, $21\frac{1}{4}$)"

# CHAPTER 5

# Head First: Hats, Caps, and Scarves

Once a purely practical consideration (there's nothing like a warm wool cap to chase away the chill), hats have become a statement of style and a reflection of the essence of the people whose heads they adorn. Standard ski caps and ribbed fisherman's caps have long been the standard, but the pattern books of old—like the department stores of today—were also filled with more fanciful styles.

Whether plain or packed with personality, a hat is one of the simplest and most satisfying projects to knit or crochet. Most require only a modest amount of yarn and an even more modest investment of time, yet offer the opportunity to try out new techniques or play with patterns on a small scale before tackling them in larger projects.

# The Snowboarder's Hat

This colorful cap first appeared as a much more subdued topper dubbed the Polo Cap. We opted to liven it up a with a textured, multicolor yarn as a complement to the plainer chunky yarn. The result is a bit of edgy attitude perfect for today's extreme winter sports.

CROCHET **EASY**

## SIZES

S (M/L)

**Circumference** 19 1/2 (22)" [49.5 (56) cm]

**Note** Before beginning pattern, circle all numbers pertaining to your size for ease in working.

## MATERIALS

(5) LION BRAND Landscapes
1 3/4 oz (50 g) 55 yd (50 m) Ball
50% Wool, 50% Acrylic

• 3 balls #279 Deep Sea (MC) or color of your choice

(5) LION BRAND Wool-Ease Chunky
5 oz (140 g) 153 yd (150 m) Ball
80% Acrylic, 20% Wool

• 1 ball #109 Royal Blue (CC) or color of your choice

• Sizes K-10.5 and N-13 (6.5 and 9 mm) crochet hooks OR SIZE TO OBTAIN GAUGE

• Scrap of contrasting yarn to be used as a marker

## GAUGE

11.5 sts + 11 rounds = 4" (10 cm) in 2-color single crochet on smaller hook.
8.5 sc + 10.5 rounds = 4" (10 cm) with MC on larger hook.
BE SURE TO CHECK YOUR GAUGE.

## HAT

**Crown** With CC and smaller hook, ch 5; join with slip stitch to form ring.

**Round 1** Work 14 sc in ring. Mark beg of round and work in a spiral.

**Round 2** (1 sc CC, 1 sc MC) around.

**Round 3** *Work 2 sc CC in first st, 1 sc MC in next st; repeat from * around—21 sc.

**Round 4** *Work 1 sc CC in first st, 2 sc CC in next st, 1 sc MC in next st; repeat from * around—28 sc.

**Rounds 5–8** Continue in pattern, working 2 sc CC in st preceding MC and working 1 MC in the MC st of previous round—56 sc.

**Round 9 (Size M/L only)** Continue in pattern as established—63 sc.

**Round 10** *Work 6 (7) sc CC, 2 sc MC; repeat from * around.

**Round 11** *Work 5 (6) sc CC, 3 sc MC; repeat from * around.

Continue in this manner, working 1 fewer sc in CC and 1 more sc in MC, until 1 sc CC remains in each repeat.

**Next round** Change to larger hook and MC only, decreasing 13 sts evenly spaced around—43 (50) sc.

Work even in MC until Hat measures 8 1/2" (21.5 cm) from beg (or desired length to brim turn-up).

**Brim** Turn Hat inside out. With WS facing, sc in back loop of each sc around. Work even in sc for 2 1/2" (6.5 cm).

## FINISHING

Fasten off. Weave in ends.

# The Hockey Cap

Sturdily crocheted, this classic cap has warmed the ears of many a young man engaged in outdoor pursuits. We left off the pompom that trimmed the original, but the basic bones of the design remain the same. Worked in team colors, it would be the perfect way to show off some school spirit. Go team!

CROCHET **EASY**

## SIZE

S/M (M/L)

**Circumference** 20 1/4 (22)" [51.5 (56) cm]

**Note** Before beginning pattern, circle all numbers pertaining to your size for ease in working.

## MATERIALS

**5** LION BRAND Wool-Ease Chunky

*5 oz (140 g) 153 yd (140 m) Ball*

*80% Acrylic, 20% Wool*

- 1 ball #152 Charcoal (MC)
- 1 ball #109 Royal Blue (CC) or colors of your choice
- Size K-10.5 (6.5 mm) crochet hook OR SIZE TO OBTAIN GAUGE
- Scrap of contrasting yarn to be used as a marker

## GAUGE

11 sc + 12 rounds = 4" (10 cm).

BE SURE TO CHECK YOUR GAUGE.

## CAP

With MC, ch 3; join with slip stitch to form ring.

**Round 1** Ch 1, work 7 sc in ring. Mark beg of round and work in a spiral.

**Round 2** Work 2 sc in each sc around—14 sc.

**Round 3** *Work 2 sc in first st, 1 sc in next st; repeat from * 6 more times—21 sc.

**Round 4** *Work 2 sc in first st, 1 sc in next 2 sts; repeat from * 6 more times—28 sc.

**Rounds 5–8** Continue in pattern, working 2 sc in first st and one additional sc in each repeat for each succeeding round—56 sc.

**Round 9 (Size M/L only)** Increase 5 sc evenly spaced around—61 sc.

Work even until Cap measures 7 1/2 (8)" [19 (20.5) cm] from beginning. Change to CC and work even in sc for 3 (3 1/2)" [7.5 (9) cm] or desired length. Fasten off.

## FINISHING

**Band edging** With MC, slip stitch in back loop of each st around. Fasten off. Weave in ends.

# The Walking Hat and Scarf

Ladies seeking a breath of fresh air would wrap themselves up in this smart fringe- and pompom-trimmed set before venturing into the cold. We changed the stripe pattern and mixed up the color for a more modern look, then replaced the pompoms with pretty crocheted flowers for a girlish touch.

CROCHET **EASY +**

## SIZE

One size

**Circumference** 21" (53.5 cm)

**Scarf** 12" x 75" (30.5 x 190.5 cm)

## MATERIALS

(4) LION BRAND Wool-Ease

*3 oz (85 g) 197 yd (180 m) Ball*

*80% Acrylic, 20 % Wool*

- 3 balls #403 Mushroom (MC)
- 1 ball #126 Chocolate Brown (A)
- 1 ball #146 Lilac (B)
- 1 ball #123 Seaspray (C)
  or colors of your choice
- Size K-10.5 (6.5 mm) crochet hook
  OR SIZE TO OBTAIN GAUGE
- Large-eyed, blunt needle

## GAUGE

13 sts + 12 rows = 4" (10 cm) in Apple Seed st.

BE SURE TO CHECK YOUR GAUGE.

## PATTERN STITCH

**APPLE SEED (Multiple of 2 sts + 1)**

**Row 1** Ch 1, *single crochet through back loop of first stitch, sc through front loop of next st; repeat from *, ending single crochet through back loop; turn. Repeat Row 1 for Apple Seed stitch.

# hat

## CROWN

With MC, ch 54.

**Row 1** Sc in 2nd ch from hook and in each ch across; turn—53 sc.
Work Apple Seed Stitch back and forth until piece measures 10½" (26.5 cm). Fasten off. Fold in half with right sides tog so that piece measures about 10½" x 8" (26.5 x 20.5 cm), and slip stitch together along each side.
**Band** With WS facing and A, work 69 sc around brim edge; join with slip stitch to beg sc; turn.
**Next row** Work Apple Seed Stitch across; join with slip stitch to beg sc; turn. Repeat this row until Band measures 3" (7.5 cm). Fasten off.
**Band edging** With RS facing and B, slip stitch through back loop of each st around. Fasten off.

## FLOWER—MAKE 2

With B, ch 3, join with slip stitch to form ring.
**Round 1** Ch 1, work 10 sc into ring; join with slip stitch to front loop of first sc.
**Round 2** Working in front loops only, (hdc, dc) in same loop as slip stitch, (dc, hdc, slip stitch) in next st, [(slip st, hdc, dc) in next st, (dc, hdc, slip stitch) in next st] 4 times; join with slip stitch to beg hdc.
**Round 3** Working this round behind last row, in the back loops only of

Round 1, (slip stitch, ch 1, sc, dc, 2 tr) in first loop, (2 tr, dc, sc) in next loop, [(sc, dc, 2 tr) in next loop, (2 tr, dc, sc) in next loop] 4 times; join with slip stitch to beg sc. Fasten off.

Fold points of Crown down to top of Band. Sew one Flower over each point, securing point to body of Hat.

# scarf

With MC, ch 40.

**Row 1** Sc in 2nd ch from hook and in each ch across; turn—39 sc.

Begin Apple Seed Stitch and work 13 more rows with MC.

Work color stripes as follows:

2 rows A, 2 rows B, 2 rows A, 2 rows C, 2 rows A, 2 rows B, 2 rows A, 2 rows C, 2 rows A, 2 rows B, 2 rows A.

Work center of Scarf in MC for 51" (129.5 cm).

Repeat color stripe sequence. End with 14 rows MC. Fasten off.

**Fringe** For each fringe, cut 5 strands of A, B, or C, each 11" (28 cm) long. Fold strands in half and, with crochet hook, pull fold through Scarf, forming a loop. Pull ends of fringe through this loop. Pull to tighten. Attach fringe evenly along short ends of Scarf in same color order as for color stripes. Trim ends evenly.

# The Saucily Sophisticated Hat

At once vintage and in vogue, this cool crocheted hat injects a bit of playfulness into the mundane task of combatting the cold. Worked as a simple rectangle, then gathered at the top to shape the crown, this timeless charmer is finished with a trio of plump pompoms.

CROCHET **EASY**

## SIZE

S/M (M/L)

**Circumference** 20³/₄ (22¹/₂)" [52.5 (57) cm]

**Note** Before beginning pattern, circle all numbers pertaining to your size for ease in working.

## MATERIALS

🧶 LION BRAND Wool-Ease

*3 oz (85 g) 197 yd (180 m) Ball*
*80% Acrylic, 20% Wool*

- 1 ball #138 Cranberry (MC)
- 1 ball #153 Black (CC)
  or colors of your choice
- Sizes J-10 and K-10.5 (6 and 6.5 mm) crochet hooks OR SIZE TO OBTAIN GAUGE
- Scraps of contrasting yarn to be used as markers
- Large-eyed, blunt needle

## GAUGE

17 sc + 16 rounds = 4" (10 cm) on smaller hook.

15 sc + 13 rounds = 4" (10 cm) on larger hook.

BE SURE TO CHECK YOUR GAUGE.

## HAT

### Crown

With MC and smaller hook, ch 3; join with slip stitch to form ring.

**Round 1** Ch 1, work 8 sc into ring. Mark beg of round and work in a spiral.

**Round 2** *Work 2 sc in first st, 1 sc in next st; repeat from * 3 more times—12 sc.

**Round 3** *Work 3 sc between first and 2nd sts, sc in next 3 sts; repeat from * 3 more times—24 sc. Mark center st of each corner increase.

**Rounds 4–8 (Inc Round)** Sc in each st around, working 3 sc in each marked center st—64 sc.

Work Inc Round every other round 3 (4) times—88 (96) sc.

Work even until Hat measures 8 (8¹/₂)" [20.5 (21.5) cm] from beg, or desired length to brim turn-up.

**Turning round** Turn Hat inside out. With WS facing, sc in back loop of each sc around.

### Brim

Change to larger hook. Work even in sc, working 4 rounds MC, 2 rounds CC, 2 rounds MC, 1 round CC, 3 rounds MC.

**Last round** With MC, slip st in back loop of each sc around. Fasten off.

## FINISHING

Make three 3" (7.5 cm) pompoms, 1 in MC and 2 in CC: Cut a piece of cardboard the length of which is approximately the circumference of the desired pompom. Cut slits on each side in the center, leaving a narrow piece between the slits. **1.** Wrap yarn around the cardboard 100–200 times (the more wraps, the fluffier the pompom). **2.** Take a separate piece of yarn and tie tightly around the bundle of wraps at the slits. Cut the tops and bottoms of wraps and slip out the cardboard. **3.** Trim the ends and fluff.

Attach to Brim at beg of rounds as pictured. Weave in ends.

# The Alpine Toque

Crocheted in a chunky stitch pattern that's a hot property by today's fashion standards, this tassel-trimmed hat needed only a change of yarn to bring it entirely up to date. We chose a bulky but lightweight variegated wool blend in a warm, woodsy mix of golds, greens, and blues.

**CROCHET EASY**

### SIZE

S/M (M/L)

**Circumference** 22 (24)" [56 (61) cm]

**Note** Before beginning pattern, circle all numbers pertaining to your size for ease in working.

### MATERIALS

**(5)** LION BRAND Landscapes

*1³/4 oz (50 g) 55 yd (50 m) Ball*

*50% Wool, 50% Acrylic*

- 3 balls #275 Autumn Trails or color of your choice
- Size N-13 (9 mm) crochet hook OR SIZE TO OBTAIN GAUGE
- Small amounts of coordinating yarns for tassels
- Scrap of contrasting yarn to be used as a marker
- Large-eyed, blunt needle

### GAUGE

4 Puff Stitches + 6 rounds = 4" (10 cm).
BE SURE TO CHECK YOUR GAUGE.

### STITCH EXPLANATION

**Puff Stitch** Yarn over, draw up a loop through space between stitches, yarn over, draw up another loop through same space, yarn over and pull through all 5 loops on hook, chain 1.

### TOQUE

Ch 4; join with slip stitch to form ring.

**Round 1** Ch 2, work 13 hdc in ring—14 hdc. Mark beg of round and work in a spiral.

**Round 2** *Work 2 Puff Stitches in first hdc, 1 Puff Stitch in next 6 hdc; repeat from * 1 more time—16 Puff Stitches.

**Round 3** *Work 2 Puff Stitches in first space, 1 Puff Stitch in next 3 spaces; repeat from * 3 more times—20 sts.

**Round 4** *Work 2 Puff Stitches in first space, 1 Puff Stitch in next 9 spaces; repeat from * 1 more time—22 sts.

**Round 5 (Size M/L only)** *Work 2 Puff Stitches in first space, 1 Puff Stitch in next 10 spaces; repeat from * 1 more time—24 sts.

Work even in Puff Stitch until Toque measures 12" (30.5 cm) or desired length. Fasten off.

### FINISHING

Leaving a 25" (63.5 cm) tail, ch 13.

**Row 1** Dc in nub in back of 4th ch from hook and in each nub across; turn—11 dc.

**Row 2** Ch 1, sc in each st across. Fasten off, leaving a 12" (30.5 cm) tail.

**Row 3** Turn work. Using first tail, sc in each st across.

Using 2nd tail, sew strip to top of crown along the increase line.

**Tassels** Using coordinating yarn, make three 5" (12.5 cm) tassels: Cut a piece of cardboard to the desired length of tassel. Wrap yarn around 25 or more times (the more wraps, the bigger the tassel). Cut a piece of yarn 18" (46 cm) long and thread doubled onto large-eyed, blunt needle.

**1.** Insert needle under all strands at upper end of cardboard. Pull tightly and knot securely near strands. Cut yarn loops at lower edge of cardboard. **2.** Cut a piece of yarn 12" (30.5 cm) long and wrap tightly around loops 1$^1$/$_2$" (4 cm) below top knot to form tassel neck. Knot securely; thread ends onto needle and weave ends to center of tassel. Trim bottom ends evenly.

Fold top of Toque over and sew tassel strip to crown to anchor. If desired, tack turned-up brim to crown. Weave in ends.

# The Feather Cap

With a wink and a nod to the grand dames of London, Paris, and New York, this fine "feathered" hat makes a sassy style statement. Crocheted in plush chenille yarn for an even richer look, it's fun to make and to wear.

## CROCHET INTERMEDIATE

### SIZE

Adult—one size

**Circumference** Adjustable for 21–23" (53.5–58.5 cm)

### MATERIALS

(6) LION BRAND Chenille Thick & Quick

*5.6 oz (158 g) 100 yd (90 m) Skein*

*81% Acrylic, 9% Rayon*

- 1 skein #155 Champagne (MC) or color of your choice

(5) LION BRAND Lion Suede

*3 oz (85 g) 122 yd (110 m) Ball*

*100% Polyester*

- 1 ball #153 Ebony (CC) or color of your choice
- Sizes N-13 (9 mm) and G-6 (4 mm) crochet hooks OR SIZE TO OBTAIN GAUGE
- Scraps of contrasting yarn to be used as markers
- 22-gauge craft store floral wire
- Floral stem tape, white
- Wire cutter
- Heavy black sewing thread and needle

### GAUGE

8 sts + 7 rounds = 4" (10 cm) in cluster pattern with MC on larger hook.

14 sc = 4" (10 cm) with CC on smaller hook.

BE SURE TO CHECK YOUR GAUGE.

### STITCH EXPLANATION

**CL** (sc2tog cluster) Insert hook into top of next cluster (2 loose loops behind CL), draw up a loop, insert hook into next chain-1 (the chain itself, not the chain-1 space), draw up a loop, yarn over and draw through all 3 loops on hook.

### FEATHER—MAKE 2

Cut a 24" (61 cm) length of wire and straighten by smoothing with fingers. Wrap floral stem tape firmly around wire to cover with a light layer, leaving 2" (5 cm) uncovered at each end. Bend wire into a 12" (30.5 cm) long narrow oval, with sharp bends at each side, bringing the two uncovered ends to overlap in the middle. Wrap tape around ends to join, wrapping the cut ends heavily so they don't poke out. The tape remains tacky and helps grab the yarn so it doesn't gap or slide. Work sts of feather firmly around wire oval just as you would a ring, trying not to bend the wire as you work.

With MC and larger hook, ch 25. Beg at one bent end of oval (quill of feather), working over wire each time, insert hook into oval and into 2nd ch from hook, draw up a loop, yarn over, and complete sc. Sc in next 2 ch, hdc in next ch, dc in next 18 ch, hdc in next ch, 3 sc in last ch (tip of feather); working in spare loops of ch, hdc in next loop, dc in next 18 loops, hdc in next loop, sc in next 2 loops, 2 sc in same ch as beg; join with slip stitch in beg sc. Fasten off. Weave in ends.

### HAT

With MC and larger hook, ch 2.

**Round 1 (RS)** 6 sc in 2nd ch from hook, place marker and continue in rounds.

**Round 2** (2 sc in next sc) 6 times—12 sc.

**Round 3** (Sc in next sc, 2 sc in next sc) 6 times—18 sc.

**Rounds 4–8** Work in pattern as established, inc 6 sc each round—48 sc.

Join with slip stitch in beg sc.

**Round 9** Ch 1, sc2tog (first sc and next sc—*CL made*), ch 1, (sc2tog, ch 1) 23 times; join with slip stitch in beg sc—24 CL.

**Rounds 10–14** Ch 1, sc2tog (first st and next ch-1), ch 1, (CL, ch 1) 23 times; join with slip stitch in top of beg CL. After last round, turn.

**Round 15 (WS)** Ch 1, skip slip stitch, (sc in next ch, sc in next CL) 24 times; join with slip stitch in beg sc; turn—48 sc.

**Rounds 16–17** Ch 1, sc in each sc around; turn.

**Round 18 (RS)** Ch 1, skip slip stitch, (CL, ch 1) 24 times. Remove last loop from hook (to be used in Brim Row 3).

BRIM

**Row 1** With RS facing and larger hook, skip next 6 CL, join MC with slip stitch in next ch-1, ch 1, (CL, ch 1) 9 times, slip stitch in next CL; turn.

**Row 2** Skip slip stitch, (CL, ch 1) 9 times, slip stitch in same ch as beg. Fasten off.

**Row 3** Pick up dropped loop, (CL, ch 1) 24 times; join with slip stitch in top of beg CL. Fasten off.

## BAND

With CC and smaller hook, ch 77.

**Round 1** 2 sc in 2nd ch from hook, sc in next 74 ch, 4 sc in last ch, sc in 74 spare loops of ch, 2 sc in same ch as beg; join with slip stitch in beg sc; turn—156 sc.

**Round 2 (RS)** Ch 1, skip slip stitch, 2 sc in next 2 sc, sc in next 70 sc, [dc in next sc, tr in next sc, dtr in next sc, 3 dtr in next 6 sc, dtr in next sc, tr in next sc, dc in next sc] (medallion made), sc in next 70 sc, 2 sc in last 2 sc; join with slip stitch in beg sc—172 sts. Fasten off.

## FINISHING

With RS facing, hold medallion to the right of the little side Brim of the Hat. Wrap Band to front around the Brim, around the back of Hat, then bring the end under medallion, aligning Band even with rows of sc just above where the edge begins to roll to outside. Pin overlapping ends to Hat and try on for fit, keeping medallion in position and adjusting the end underneath. Pin Band to Hat in a few places, easing in fullness. With needle and heavy black thread, keeping round medallion completely free, sew across width of Band securely on each side of the little side Brim, then sew across other end lapped under medallion.

Hold quills of feathers tog, with feathers in a V, roughly in position as pictured. Sew a few sts across quill ends through both thicknesses, catching wires. Hold quill ends against right side of Hat, positioned as pictured. Cover bottom of feathers with medallion; sew through medallion, feathers, end of Band underneath, and Hat in a circle about midway between center and edge of medallion, catching dtrs of medallion and wires of feathers as much as possible.

Roll edge of Hat to outside, very carefully bend feathers into shape (it's difficult to unbend wires once bent). The feathers should be bent so that they are slightly curved and lean toward the back of the hat.

# The Skating Cap

Thick yarn and a simple stitch pattern partner up for a cool cap with unisex appeal. Stitched in a solid or two-toned twist, it crochets up in no time. It's the ideal project for a new crocheter or a more experienced stitcher looking for a fast-finishing project.

CROCHET **EASY**

### SIZES

S/M (M/L)

**Circumference** 21 (23)" [53.5 (58.5) cm]

**Note** Before beginning pattern, circle all numbers pertaining to your size for ease in working.

### MATERIALS

LION BRAND Wool-Ease Thick & Quick
6 oz (170 g) 108 yd (98 m) Ball
80% Acrylic, 20% Wool

- 1 ball #152 Pewter or color of your choice
- Size P-15 (10 mm) crochet hook OR SIZE TO OBTAIN GAUGE
- Scrap of contrasting yarn to be used as a marker

### GAUGE

4 Bean Stitches + 4 rounds = 4" (10 cm).

BE SURE TO CHECK YOUR GAUGE.

### STITCH EXPLANATION

#### BEAN STITCH

Draw up a loop through first space, yarn over, draw up a loop through same space, yarn over, draw up a loop through same space, yarn over, and draw through all 6 loops on hook, chain 1.

### PATTERN STITCH

#### BRIM STITCH

**Round 1** Draw up a loop through first space, draw up a loop through top of next st, draw up a loop through next space, yarn over and draw through all 4 loops on hook, ch 1; *draw up a loop through same space as previous loop, draw up a loop through top of next st, draw up a loop through next space, yarn over and draw through all 4 loops on hook, ch 1; repeat from * to end of round.

**Round 2** Draw up a loop through first space, draw up a loop between 2nd and 3rd sts of cluster on previous round, draw up a loop through next space, yarn over and draw through all 4 loops on hook, ch 1; *draw up a loop through same space as previous loop, draw up a loop between 2nd and 3rd sts of cluster on previous round, draw up a loop through next space, yarn over and draw through all 4 loops on hook, ch 1; repeat from * to end of round.

Repeat Round 2 for Brim Stitch.

### CAP

**Crown** Ch 5; join with slip stitch to form ring.

**Round 1** Work 7 Bean Stitches in ring. Mark beg of round and work in a spiral.

**Round 2** Work 2 Bean Stitches in each space around—14 Bean Stitches.

**Rounds 3 and 5** Work even.

**Round 4** *Work 2 Bean Stitches in first space, 1 Bean Stitch in next space; repeat from * 6 more times—21 Bean Stitches.

**Round 6** Inc 0 (2) Bean Stitches evenly spaced around—21 (23) Bean

Stitches.

Work even until Cap measures 8 (9)" [20.5 (23) cm] from beg, or desired length to Brim turn-up.

**Brim** Turn Cap inside out. With WS facing, work in Brim stitch for 3$\frac{1}{2}$" (9 cm) or desired length. Fasten off. Weave in ends.

# The Nouveau French Beret

Crown yourself in a halo of fluffy, furry yarn with this jaunty crocheted beret. Taking a cue from the original (which was stitched in soft mohair), we chose a color-flecked Fun Fur. The result is a playful topper with plenty of ooh-la-la to spare.

CROCHET **EASY**

## SIZE

S/M (M/L)

**Circumference** 18 1/2" (47 cm) at opening, 29 1/2 (33 1/4)" [75 (84.5) cm] at widest point

**Note** Before beginning pattern, circle all numbers pertaining to your size for ease in working.

## MATERIALS

LION BRAND Wool-Ease Chunky
*5 oz (140 g) 153 yd (140 m) Ball*
*80% Acrylic, 20% Wool*
- 1 ball #107 Bluebell (MC)
  or color of your choice

LION BRAND Fun Fur
*1 1/2 oz (40 g) 57 yd (52 m) Ball*
*100% Polyester\*
- 3 balls #208 Tropical (CC)
  or color of your choice
- Size P-15 (10 mm) crochet hook
  OR SIZE TO OBTAIN GAUGE
- Scrap of contrasting yarn to be used
  as a marker

## GAUGE

6.5 sc + 8 rounds = 4" (10 cm) with 1 strand of MC and 2 strands of CC held together.
BE SURE TO CHECK YOUR GAUGE.

## BERET

**Crown** With 1 strand of MC and 2 strands of CC held together, ch 4; join with slip st to form ring.

**Round 1** Ch 1, work 6 sc in ring. Mark beg of round and work in a spiral.

**Round 2** Work 2 sc in each sc around—12 sc.

**Round 3** *Work 2 sc in first st, 1 sc in next st; repeat from * 5 more times—18 sc.

**Round 4** *Work 2 sc in first st, 1 sc in next 2 sts; repeat from * 5 more times—24 sc.

**Rounds 5–8** Continue in pattern as established, working 2 sc in first st and 1 additional sc in each repeat each succeeding round—48 sc.

**Round 9 (Size M/L only)** Continue in pattern as established—54 sc.
Work even for 4 rounds.

**Dec for Band**

**Next round** (Size M/L only) *8 sc, skip one st; repeat from * 5 more times—48 sc.

**Next round** *7 sc, skip one st; repeat from * 5 more times—42 sc.
Continue in this manner, decreasing 6 sts every round, 2 more times—30 sc.

Try on Beret. If fit is loose, change to a smaller hook; if snug, change to a larger hook. Work 2 rounds even. Fasten off.
Weave in ends.

# The Calot Cap

This striking cap is so easy to knit we just couldn't pass it by. We replaced the brightly hued mohair of the original with a slightly more sophisticated—but equally playful— Fun Fur, flecked with tiny poms of color.

KNIT **EASY**

## SIZES
S/M (M/L)

**Circumference** 21 (22 3/4)" [53.5 (58) cm]

**Note** Before beginning pattern, circle all numbers pertaining to your size for ease in working.

## MATERIALS
(6) LION BRAND Fancy Fur

*1 3/4 oz (50 g) 39 yd (35m) Ball*

*55% Polyamide, 45% Polyester*

- 2 balls #254 Stained Glass Black or color of your choice
- Size 10.5 (6.5 mm) double-pointed needles OR SIZE TO OBTAIN GAUGE
- Large-eyed, blunt needle

## GAUGE
9.5 sts + 11 rounds = 4" (10 cm) in Stockinette stitch (knit every row).
BE SURE TO CHECK YOUR GAUGE.

## HAT
Cast on 50 (54) sts. Join,

being careful not to twist. Work even in St st for 8 1/2" (21.5 cm).

**Dec Round 1** Knit 2 together around—25 (27) sts.

Work 3 rounds even.

**Dec Round 2** K 1, (k2tog) around—13 (14) sts.

Work 3 rounds even.

**Dec Round 3** K 1 (0), (k2tog) around—7 sts.

Work 2 rounds even.

Break off bobbly thread and, using furry portion of yarn only, pull through remaining sts and tighten. Weave in ends.

Turn up 1" (2.5 cm) of bottom roll and, using furry portion of yarn only, tack down loosely.

# The Cozy Elegant Set

## SIZE

**MUFF**

**Circumference** 21½″ (54.5 cm)

**Length** 18″ (45.5 cm)

**SCARF**

4″ x 62½″ (10 x 159 cm)

**HAT**

S/M (M/L)

**Circumference** 20 (22)″ [51 (56) cm]

**Note** Before beginning pattern, circle all numbers pertaining to your size for ease in working.

## MATERIALS

⑥ LION BRAND Chenille
Thick & Quick
5.6 oz (158 g) 100 yd (90 m) Skein
91% Acrylic, 9% Rayon

- 3 skeins #153 Black (MC)
- 1 skein #239 Garnet Print (CC) or colors of your choice
- Sizes P-15 (10 mm) and N-13 (9 mm) crochet hooks OR SIZE TO OBTAIN GAUGE
- Scrap of contrasting yarn to be used as a marker
- Polar Fleece for lining Muff
- Sewing needle and thread to match Polar Fleece
- Large-eyed, blunt needle

## GAUGE

6.5 sts + 4 rounds = 4″ (10 cm) in Muff Stitch on smaller hook.

6 hdc + 5 rounds = 4″ (10 cm) on larger hook.

8 hdc + 6 rounds = 4″ (10 cm) on smaller hook.

BE SURE TO CHECK YOUR GAUGE.

This age-old trio translates well into an updated mode with a modern-day plush chenille yarn. The new yarn allows the set to be finished more quickly using big crochet hooks. Whether you wear all three items together or just choose individual pieces, you'll be sure to make a dramatic statement.

CROCHET **EASY +**

### PATTERN STITCH

#### MUFF STITCH

**Round 1** Ch 2, yarn over, draw up a loop through 2nd chain from hook, draw up a loop through first stitch in previous round, yarn over and draw through all 4 loops on hook, *yarn over, draw up a loop through the back loop of last loop made in previous stitch, draw up a loop through next stitch, yarn over and draw through all 4 loops on hook; repeat from * around. Join with slip stitch to top of beg ch-2. Repeat Round 1 for Muff Stitch.

### MUFF

With CC and smaller hook, ch 36; join with slip stitch to form ring. Work in Muff Stitch, working into each ch around—35 sts.

Continuing in Muff Stitch, work 2 more rounds CC, 11 rounds MC, and 3 rounds CC.

With MC, ch 1, sc in each st around; join with slip stitch to beg sc. Fasten off.

Join MC to beg ch. Ch 1, sc in spare loop of each ch around; join with slip stitch to beg sc. Fasten off.

**Finishing**

Turn Muff inside out. Cut a piece of Polar Fleece about ½″ (1.25 cm) shorter and same width as the circumference of the Muff. Using sewing needle and matching thread, sew Polar Fleece to each end. Sew long seam of Polar Fleece lining. Turn right side out.

## SCARF

With MC and larger hook, ch 5; join with slip stitch to form ring.

**Round 1** Ch 2, work 11 hdc in ring—12 sts. Mark beg of round and work in a spiral.

Hdc in each st around until piece measures 4" (10 cm). Change to CC and work 3 rounds. Change to MC and work even until piece measures 56" (142 cm) from end of CC stripe. Change to CC and work 3 rounds. Change to MC and work even until piece measures 4" (10 cm) from end of second CC stripe. Break off yarn, leaving 12" (30.5 cm) tail.

### Finishing

Thread tail through all sts and pull to tighten. Fasten off securely. Make small tassels with MC and CC (see page 114) and fasten to each end of Scarf.

With MC, smaller hook, and leaving a 6" (15 cm) tail, ch 4; join with slip stitch to form ring.

**Round 1** Ch 2, work 11 hdc in ring; join with slip stitch to top of beg ch-2 —12 sts.

**Round 2** Ch 2, hdc in first st, 2 hdc in each st around; join with slip stitch to top of beg ch-2—24 sts.

**Round 3** Ch 2, 2 hdc in next st, *hdc in next st, 2 hdc in next st; repeat from * around; join with slip stitch to top of beg ch-2—36 sts.

**Round 4 (Size S/M only)** Ch 2, hdc in next 7 sts, 2 hdc in next st, *hdc in next 8 sts, 2 hdc in next st; repeat from * around; join with slip stitch to top of beg ch-2—40 sts.

**Round 4 (Size M/L only)** Ch 2, hdc in next 3 sts, 2 hdc in next st, hdc in next 3 sts, 2 hdc in next st, *hdc in next 4 sts, 2 hdc in next st, hdc in next 3 sts, 2 hdc in next st; repeat from * around; join with slip stitch to top of beg ch-2—44 sts.

**Rounds 5–7** Ch 2, hdc in each st around; join with slip stitch to top of beg ch-2.

**Round 8** Ch 2 CC, 2 hdc CC, 1 hdc MC, *3 hdc CC, 1 hdc MC; repeat from * around; join with slip stitch to top of beg ch-2.

**Round 9** Ch 2 MC, 2 hdc CC, 1 hdc MC, *1 hdc MC, 2 hdc CC, 1 hdc MC; repeat from * around; join with slip stitch to top of beg ch-2.

**Round 10** Ch 2 MC, 1 hdc MC, 1 hdc CC, 1 hdc MC, *2 hdc MC, 1 hdc CC, 1 hdc MC; repeat from * around; join with slip stitch to top of beg ch-2. Fasten off CC.

**Round 11** With MC, ch 2, hdc in each st around; join with slip stitch to top of beg ch-2.

**Round 12** Ch 1, reverse sc in each st around; join with slip stitch to beg sc. Fasten off.

**Finishing**

Thread tail through sts at top and pull to tighten. Fasten off securely. Weave in ends.

# CHAPTER 6

# Oh, Baby!
# Little Things
# We Love

Think of knitting, and the image that most often comes to mind (save perhaps that of granny in her rocker) is that of a expectant mother, gently humming lullabies as she patiently knits or crochets a tiny pair of booties for her baby-to-be. In days of old, by the time baby finally did make an appearance, his or her dresser drawers would already be filled with a stunning array of blankets, caps, and coats—all lovingly stitched by friends and family in gender-neutral shades of cream, yellow, and mint green.

We still love knitting and crocheting for babies. After all, the pieces are so tiny, so adorable, and so much fun to make. Booties, blankets, and bonnets are still the projects of choice, but modern moms and dads love fun yarns and bright, bold hues just as much as traditional pastels. New yarns, new colors, and easy-care fibers have opened the doors to a world of creativity and the pleasures of yarn and needles.

# The Lovely Layette

Some things are hard to improve on. Take this Linda Baby Classic bonnet, mitten, bootie, and sweater set—all too adorable for words. Rather than fuss with the styling (which, like the little one who will wear it, is perfect in our eyes), we simply decided to crochet this heirloom-quality set in a super-soft, machine-washable yarn.

## CROCHET EASY

### SIZE

Newborn–3 months

**Finished chest** 21″ (53.5 cm)

**Length** 11¼″ (28.5 cm)

### MATERIALS

(3) LION BRAND Babysoft

*5 oz (140 g) 459 yd (413 m) Ball*

*60% Acrylic, 40% Nylon*

- 2 balls #157 Pastel Yellow or color of your choice
- Size H-8 (5 mm) crochet hook OR SIZE TO OBTAIN GAUGE
- Stitch markers
- White satin ribbon, 4 yards (3.6 m) long x ½″ (13 mm) wide
- Large-eyed, blunt needle

### GAUGE

19 sc + 24 rows = 4″ (10 cm).

BE SURE TO CHECK YOUR GAUGE.

### STITCH EXPLANATION

SOLOMON'S KNOT Pull up a loop on hook about ¾″ (2 cm) long, yarn over and draw through loop as if to chain, insert hook under single thread at back of loop and single crochet tightly.

PATTERN STITCH (multiple of 3 sts + 1)

**Row 1** Ch 1, sc in first st, *work a Solomon's Knot, skip 2 sts, sc in next st; repeat from *; turn.

**Row 2** Ch 3, dc in first sc, *3 dc in next sc; repeat from *, ending with dc in last st; turn.

**Row 3** Ch 1, sc in first dc, *work a Solomon's Knot, sc in center dc of next 3-dc group; repeat from *, ending with sc in top of t-ch; turn.

**Row 4** Repeat Row 2.

Repeat Rows 3–4 for Pattern Stitch.

### SWEATER

NOTE The Sweater is worked in one piece from the top down.

Yoke Ch 57.

**Row 1 (WS)** Sc in 2nd ch from hook and in each ch across; turn—56 sc.

**Row 2** Ch 1, sc in first 12 sts (Left Front), 3 sc in next st (raglan increase point), sc in next 4 sts (Left Sleeve), 3 sc in next st, sc in next 20 sts (Back), 3 sc in next st, sc in next 4 sts (Right Sleeve), 3 sc in next st, sc in next 12 sts (Right Front); turn—64 sts. Mark the center st of each of the 4 raglan increase points.

**Rows 3–15** Ch 1, *sc in each sc to next marked st, 3 sc in marked st; repeat from * across, ending with sc to end of row; turn.

**Join Fronts and Back** Ch 1, sc in 27 sts of Left Front, ch 10 for underarm, skip 32 sts of Left Sleeve, sc in 50 sts of Back, ch 10 for underarm, skip

32 sts of Right Sleeve, sc in 27 sts of Right Front; turn—124 sts (104 sc + 20 ch).

**Skirt** Change to Pattern Stitch and work even for 8" (20.5 cm), ending with Row 4. Fasten off.

**Sleeves** With WS facing, attach yarn at center of underarm chain. Work back and forth in Pattern Stitch for 5" (12.5 cm) or desired length to Cuff, increasing one st in first st of Pattern Row 1, and ending with Pattern Row 4.

**Cuff** Ch 1, sc in first dc, *skip 1 dc, sc in next 2 dc; repeat from * across. Work 6 rows sc.

**Picot edging** *Sc in each of next 4 sts, ch 3, sc in same st as last sc; repeat from *, ending sc in last st. Fasten off.

**Finishing** Sew Sleeve and Cuff seam. With RS facing and beg on Right Front at lower edge of Yoke, work Picot edging to top of Yoke; work Back neck (for ribbon eyelets) as follows: ch 4, skip 1 sc, dc in next st, *ch 1, skip one st, dc in next st; repeat from * to end of Back neck; work Picot edging along Left Front of Yoke. At beg of Skirt, work Pattern Row 3 along Left Front, lower edge, and Right Front of Skirt; turn. Ch 1, sc in first sc, *work a Solomon's Knot, sc in next sc; repeat from * along Right Front, lower edge, and Left Front of Skirt, ending with sc in last sc. Fasten off.

Cut a 1 yard (.9 m) length of ribbon and thread through eyelets at neckline.

## BONNET

NOTE The Bonnet (not shown) begins at center back and is worked in rounds to form crown. The brim of the Bonnet is worked back and forth.

**Crown** Ch 4; join with slip stitch to form ring.

**Round 1** Work 6 sc into ring. Place marker for beg of round and work in a spiral.

**Round 2** Work 2 sc in each st around— 12 sc.

**Round 3** *Work 2 sc in first st, 1 sc in next st; repeat from * 5 more times —18 sc.

**Round 4** *Work 2 sc in first st, 1 sc in next 2 sts; repeat from * 5 more times—24 sc.

**Rounds 5–13** Continue in pattern as established, working 2 sc in first st and 1 additional sc in each repeat each succeeding round—78 sc.

**Brim** Turn. Work in Pattern Stitch across the first 5 sections (leaving the 6th unworked for back of neck). Continue to work back and forth in Pattern Stitch until there are 7 full repeats of Pattern Stitch (14 rows), ending with Pattern Row 4. Work Pattern Row 3 again.

**Last row** Ch 1, sc in first sc, *work a Solomon's Knot, sc in next sc; repeat from *, ending with sc in last sc. Fasten off.

**Neckband** Attach yarn at one side of neck and work 2 rows sc—13 sc.

**Row 3** *Sc in first 5 sts, skip one st; repeat from *, ending sc in last st. Fasten off.

Cut a 1 yard (.9 m) length of ribbon and thread through Brim on 4th repeat of Pattern Stitch.

BOOTIES—MAKE 2

NOTE The Booties begin with a rectangle for the top of the foot (instep). A chain is worked to go around the ankle and is joined to the other side of the instep. Sc is worked around 3 edges of the rectangle and across the ankle chain to form the foot. The Pattern Stitch is worked back and forth to form the Cuff.

**Instep** Ch 11. Sc in 2nd ch from hook and in each ch across; turn—10 sc. Work 9 more rows sc.

**Foot** Ch 26 (for ankle); join with slip stitch to top of Instep at opposite end. Work 1 sc in end of each row along side of Instep, sc in each beg ch at bottom of Instep, sc in end of each row along second side of Instep, sc in each ankle ch—56 sc. Work 6 more rounds sc.

**Dec round 1** *Work 5 sc, sc2tog; repeat from * around—48 sc.

**Dec round 2** *Work 4 sc, sc2tog; repeat from * around—40 sc.

**Dec round 3** *Work 3 sc, sc2tog; repeat from * around—32 sc.

**Dec round 4** *Work 2 sc, sc2tog; repeat from * around—24 sc.

**Dec round 5** *Work 1 sc, sc2tog; repeat from * around—16 sc.

Fasten off, leaving an 8" (20.5 cm) tail. Use tail to seam bottom of sole.

**Cuff** Join yarn in 13th ch of ankle ch (center back of Bootie). Work back and forth around top of Bootie in Pattern Stitch for 4 rows. Work Pattern Row 3 again.

**Last row** Ch 1, sc in first sc, *work a Solomon's Knot, sc in next sc; repeat from *, ending with sc in last sc. Fasten off, leaving an 8" (20.5

cm) tail. Using tail, sew back seam of Cuff.

Cut an 18" (45.5 cm) length of ribbon and thread through Cuff on first repeat of Pattern Stitch. Tie into bow.

MITTENS—MAKE 2

NOTE Mittens are worked from tip to Cuff.

Ch 2.

**Row 1** Work 6 sc in 2nd ch from hook. Place marker for beg of round and work in a spiral.

**Round 2** Work 2 sc in each st around—12 sc.

**Round 3** *Work 2 sc in first st, 1 sc in next st; repeat from * 5 more times—18 sc.

**Round 4** *Work 2 sc in first st, 1 sc in next 2 sts; repeat from * 5 more times—24 sc.

Work even in sc for 12 more rounds, or desired length to Cuff, increasing one st on last round.

**Cuff** Turn. Work Pattern Row 1 across. Turn. Work Pattern Row 2. Continue working in Pattern Stitch back and forth for 2 more rows. Work Pattern Row 3 again.

**Last row** Ch 1, sc in first sc, *work a Solomon's Knot, sc in next sc; repeat from *, ending with sc in last sc. Fasten off, leaving an 8" (20.5 cm) tail. Using tail, sew side seam of Cuff.

Cut an 18" (45.5 cm) length of ribbon and thread through Cuff on first repeat of Pattern Stitch. Tie into bow.

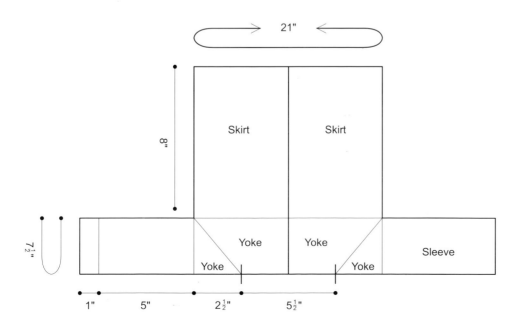

# The Baby Hat: Take 1

It's a mystery to us why this cute cap was originally dubbed the Baby Boy's Toque, so we see no reason to keep it a secret from the girls. Pick a color that flatters your little angel's coloring, disposition, and gender, and crochet away. This is the perfect baby shower gift.

CROCHET **EASY**

### SIZE

Newborn to 6 months (6 to 18 months)
**Circumference** 16½ (18)" [42 (45.5) cm]
**Note** Before beginning pattern, circle all numbers pertaining to your size for ease in working.

### MATERIALS

(3) LION BRAND Babysoft
*5 oz (140 g) 459 yd (413 m) Ball*
*60% Acrylic, 40% Nylon*
- 1 ball #143 Lavender
  or color of your choice
- Size H-8 (5 mm) crochet hook OR
  SIZE TO OBTAIN GAUGE
- Large-eyed, blunt needle

### GAUGE

24 sts + 25 rows = 4" (10 cm) in pattern st.
BE SURE TO CHECK YOUR GAUGE.

**NOTE** Hat is worked from side to side.

### HAT

Ch 46 (48).
**Row 1** Sc in 2nd ch from hook and in each ch across; turn—45 (47) sc.
**Row 2** Ch 1, sc in first st, *ch 1, skip one st, sc in next st; repeat from * across; turn.
**Row 3** Ch 1, *sc in next ch-1 space, ch 1; repeat from * across, ending sc in last ch-1 space; turn.
**Row 4** Ch 1, *sc in next ch-1 space, ch 1; repeat from * across, ending sc in t-ch; turn.
Repeat Row 4 until piece measures 16½ (18)" [42 (45.5) cm]. Fasten off.

### FINISHING

Fold rectangle in half, meeting starting ch and last row. Sew this seam for side seam. Sew one edge together for top of Hat.
**Brim** Join yarn with slip stitch at bottom of Hat.
**Row 1** Ch 1, work sc evenly spaced around bottom of Hat; join with slip stitch to beg sc; turn.
**Rows 2–9** Repeat Row 1.
Fasten off. Weave in ends.
Make 2 pompoms: Cut a piece of cardboard the length of which is approximately the circumference of the desired pompom. Cut slits on each side in the center, leaving a narrow piece between the slits. **1.** Wrap yarn around the cardboard 100–200 times (the more wraps, the fluffier the pompom). **2.** Take a separate piece of yarn and tie tightly around the bundle of wraps at the slits. Cut the tops and bottoms of wraps and slip out the cardboard. **3.** Trim the ends and fluff.
Attach pompoms to corners at top of Hat. Turn down corners and tack in place over side seam. Turn up Brim and tack in place.

# The Baby Hat: Take 2

Topped with a plush pompom, this adorable cap has a lovely old-fashioned feel. Like its cousin on the preceding page, it was originally designed for baby boys. And while it's certainly a look that can be worn by the fairer sex with equal flair, we followed the lead of the original design and crocheted it bright blue.

## CROCHET **EASY**

### SIZE

Newborn to 6 months (6 to 18 months)

**Circumference** 15 1/4 (16 3/4)" [38.5 (42.5) cm]

**Note** Before beginning pattern, circle all numbers pertaining to your size for ease in working.

### MATERIALS

**(3)** LION BRAND Babysoft

*5 oz (140 g) 459 yd (413 m) Ball*

*60% Acrylic, 40% Nylon*

- 1 ball #107 Bluebell
  or color of your choice
- Size H-8 (5 mm) crochet hook
  OR SIZE TO OBTAIN GAUGE
- Scrap of contrasting yarn to be used
  as a marker
- Large-eyed, blunt needle

### GAUGE

22 sc + 28 rounds = 4" (10 cm).
BE SURE TO CHECK YOUR GAUGE.

### HAT

Ch 3; join with slip stitch to form ring.

**Round 1** Work 7 sc in ring. Mark beg of round and work in a spiral.

**Round 2** Work 2 sc in each st around—14 sc.

**Round 3** *Work 2 sc in first st, sc in next st; repeat from * 6 more times —21 sc.

**Round 4** *Work 2 sc in first st, sc in next 2 sts; repeat from * 6 more times—28 sc.

Continue in pattern as established, working 2 sc in first st and one additional sc in each group repeat each succeeding round, until there are 10 (11) sc between increasing points—84 (91) sc.

**Next round (larger size only)** 2 sc in first st, sc in each st around—92 sc. Work even until piece measures 4 (5)" [10 (12.5) cm] or desired length to Band.

**Turning round** Turn hat inside out. With WS facing, sc in back loop of each sc around.

**Band**

**Round 1** Ch 1, sc in first st, draw up a loop in first st and each of the next 2 sts, yarn over and draw through all 4 loops on hook (Cluster made), *ch 1, draw up a loop in the same st where last loop of previous Cluster was drawn, draw up a loop in each of the next 2 sts, yarn over, and draw through all 4 loops on hook; repeat from * around, ending ch 1, sc in last st.

**Round 2** Sc in first st, sc in space, *draw up a loop in top of Cluster, draw up a loop in space, draw up a loop in next space (there is only one thread between these spaces), yarn over and draw through all 4 loops on hook, ch 1; repeat from * around.

**Round 3** Sc in first sc, draw up a loop in same st, draw up a loop in each of the next 2 spaces, yarn over and draw through all 4 loops on hook, ch 1, *draw up a loop in each of the next 3 spaces, yarn over and draw through all 4 loops on hook, ch 1; repeat from * around.

Work 3 rounds sc.

**Band edging** Slip stitch in back loop of each sc around. Fasten off. Weave in ends.

Make a pompom (see page 136) and attach to top of Hat. Turn up Band and tack in place.

# The Baby Sacque

Cozy little cardigans like these were once a part of every infant's layette. Today's tastes make the ruffled textured stitches a bit too feminine for baby boys, so we decided to knit the new version in a bold shade of pink. Divine!

KNIT with CROCHET edging **EASY**

## SIZE

6 months (12 months)

**Finished chest** 23 (25)″ [58.5 (63.5) cm]

**Length** 11 (13¼)″ [28 (33.5) cm]

**Note** Before beginning pattern, circle all numbers pertaining to your size for ease in working.

## MATERIALS

**(3)** LION BRAND Babysoft

*5 oz (140 g) 459 yd (413 m) Ball*

*60% Acrylic, 40% Nylon*

- 1 (2) balls #103 Bubblegum (MC)
- 1 ball #100 White (CC)
  or colors of your choice
- Size 6 (4 mm) knitting needles
  OR SIZE TO OBTAIN GAUGE
- Size G-6 (4 mm) crochet hook
- Stitch holders
- Large-eyed, blunt needle

## GAUGE

21 sts + 31 rows = 4″ (10 cm) in Pattern Stitch.

BE SURE TO CHECK YOUR GAUGE.

**NOTE** This cardigan is worked from side to side in one piece. Work all edge stitches in Stockinette stitch (k on RS, p on WS).

## PATTERN STITCH (multiple of 6 sts)

**Rows 1–4** *K 3, p 3; repeat from *.

**Rows 5 and 7 (RS)** Knit.

**Row 6** Purl.

**Rows 8–11** *P 3, k 3; repeat from *.

**Rows 12–14** Repeat Rows 5–7.

Repeat Rows 1–14 for pattern.

## CARDIGAN

With MC, cast on 50 (56) sts.

**Row 1** K 1 (edge st), *k 3, p 3; repeat from * to last st, k 1 (edge st). Maintaining edge sts in St St, continue in Pattern Stitch as established (beg with Row 2), until 48 (62) rows have been worked.

**Begin back and front** Cast on 33 (42) sts at beg of next 2 rows—116 (140) sts. Continue in pattern as established for 24 (26) more rows.

**Divide for neck** Work 58 (70) sts for Back; place remaining sts on holder for Front. Work even on Back sts for 42 (46) rows; place sts on holder. Slip Front sts from holder to needle—58 (70) sts. With RS facing and beg Row 5 (7) of Pattern Stitch, work even for 22 (24) rows. Bind off.

**Next row** Cast on 58 (70) sts and, with RS facing and beg Row 13 (Row 3) of Pattern Stitch, work 21 (23) rows even.

**Join back and front (WS)** Work across Front sts, then work Back sts from holder—116 (140) sts. Work 24 (26) rows even. Bind off 33 (42) sts at beg of next 2 rows—50 (56) sts. Work even for 48 (62) rows. Bind off.

## FINISHING

Using an invisible seam (see Techniques, page 188), sew side and Sleeve seams.

**Shell edging** Beg at Left Back neck, work Shell edging all around as follows:

**Round 1** With RS facing and CC, *sc in first st, skip 3 sts, 5 dc in next st, skip 3 sts; repeat from * to Front edge. Along Front edge, *sc in first row, skip 4 rows, 5 dc in next row, skip 4 rows; repeat from * to bottom edge. Continue in this way around edge, skipping 3 sts or 4 rows between Shells. Join with slip stitch to beg sc. Fasten off.

**Round 2** With RS facing, join MC at Left Back neck. Work *5 dc in next sc, sc in center of Shell; repeat from * around. Join with slip stitch to beg dc. Fasten off. Work Shell edging on Sleeve cuffs. Weave in ends.

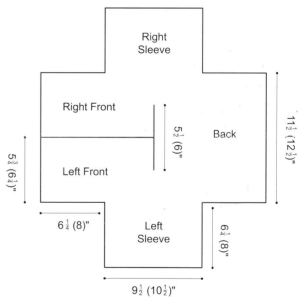

Right Sleeve

Right Front

Left Front

Back

$5\frac{1}{2}$ (6)"

$11\frac{1}{2}$ $(12\frac{1}{2})$"

$5\frac{3}{4}$ $(6\frac{1}{4})$"

$6\frac{1}{4}$ (8)"

Left Sleeve

$6\frac{1}{4}$ (8)"

$9\frac{1}{2}$ $(10\frac{1}{2})$"

# The Warm-Weather Blanket

While they certainly don't need as much bundling as their October-to-March compatriots, spring and summer babies still need a blanket to chase off the chill from air-conditioned interiors—not to mention a clean, soft spot on which to nap or play during outings to the park. Crocheted in cool, cotton-blend yarn, this simple striped throw is the perfect solution.

CROCHET **EASY**

### SIZE
32" x 38" (81.5 x 96.5 cm)

### MATERIALS
**(4)** LION BRAND Cotton-Ease

*5 oz (140 g) 236 yd (212 m) ball*

*50% Cotton, 50% Acrylic*

- 3 balls #100 White (A)
- 3 balls #123 Seaspray (B) or colors of your choice
- Size I-9 (5.5 mm) crochet hook OR SIZE TO OBTAIN GAUGE

### GAUGE
9 Clusters + 8 rows = 4" (10 cm).

BE SURE TO CHECK YOUR GAUGE.

### NOTES
Blanket is worked lengthwise.

To change colors at end of row, work previous Cluster until 4 loops on hook, drop color, pick up new color from underneath, complete Cluster with new color. Unused strand may be carried up side of work, or yarn may be fastened off at end of each color stripe.

### STITCH EXPLANATIONS

**Note** The eye of a Cluster is made by the ch-1 that closes that Cluster.

**Cluster**

**First leg** Insert hook in ch-1 eye just made, draw up a loop.

**2nd leg** Insert hook in the strand in back of the 3rd leg of last Cluster made, draw up a loop. Skip loops at top of next Cluster.

**3rd leg** Insert hook in the next eye of Cluster in previous row, draw up a loop. Yarn over and draw through all 4 loops on hook.

**Shell** (3 dc, ch 2, 3 dc) in same stitch.

**Corner Shell** (4 dc, ch 2, 4 dc) in same corner stitch.

### BLANKET

With B, ch 163.

**Foundation Row** Skip first ch from hook, draw a loop in each of the next 2 ch, yarn over and draw through all 3 loops on hook (*beg Cluster made*), (ch 1, draw a loop in the eye of ch-1 just made, draw a loop through strand in back of leg of previous Cluster made, skip next base ch, draw a loop through next base ch, yarn over and draw through all 4 loops on hook) across; turn.

**Pattern Row** Ch 3, skip first ch from hook, draw up a loop in each of the next 2 ch, draw up a loop through first eye of Cluster in previous row, yarn over and draw through all 4 loops on hook, (ch 1, Cluster) across, placing 3rd leg of ending Cluster in the unworked top ch of t-ch; turn.

Work Pattern Row twice more with B. Repeat Pattern Row, alternating 4 rows A, 4 rows B, until there are 15 stripes (8 of B, 7 of A). Fasten off B.

**Shell edge** With RS facing and A, ch 3, 3 dc in same corner st, (skip next ch-1, skip top of next Cluster, skip next ch-1, sc in top of next Cluster, skip next ch-1, skip top of next Cluster, skip next ch-1, Shell in top of next Cluster) 20 times across, working Corner Shell in last st; work across short side with (sc in center of color stripe, Shell in end of color stripe) 15 times across, working Corner Shell in last st; work across foundation row with (skip next unworked base ch, sc in next unworked base ch, skip next unworked base ch, Shell in next unworked base ch) 20 times, working Corner Shell in last st; work second short side as for first, working 4 dc in last st (same st as beg), ch 2, slip stitch in top of beg ch. Fasten off. Weave in ends.

# The Crocheted Kimono

Worked in open, lacy stitches, this sweet top is still one of the most elegant baby garments we've ever seen. We swapped the original satin ribbon ties for a less frilly but equally feminine cord tie; easy-care yarn makes it as pretty as it is practical.

## CROCHET INTERMEDIATE

### SIZE

Newborn (6 months, 12 months)
**Finished chest** 16 (20, 22)" [40.5 (51, 56) cm]
**Note** Before beginning pattern, circle all numbers pertaining to your size for ease in working.

### MATERIALS

**3** LION BRAND Babysoft
*5 oz (140 g) 459 yd (413 m) Ball*
*60% Acrylic, 40% Nylon*

- 1 ball #099 Cream
  or color of your choice
- Size G-6 (4 mm) crochet hook OR
  SIZE TO OBTAIN GAUGE
- Satin ribbon, 1½" (4 cm) wide, 1 yard
  (1 m) long (optional)

### GAUGE

17 sts + 8 rows = 4" (10 cm) in Yoke Pattern.
4 shells + 7 rows = 4" (10 cm) in Body Pattern.
BE SURE TO CHECK YOUR GAUGE.

### NOTES

This garment begins at the bottom of the Back Yoke and works up to the neck. Each Front Yoke is then worked from the shoulder down. The bottom of the Fronts and Back Yoke are joined at the underarm to form the armhole. The Body is worked from the bottom of the Yoke down. Sleeves are then worked from the armhole down.

Yoke pattern alternates WS rows of double crochet with RS rows of double crochet Crosses worked through the back loop only.

### STITCH EXPLANATIONS

**Cross** Skip next st, dc through back loop of next st. Reaching behind dc just made, dc through back loop of same st as front leg of previous Cross.
**Shell** (2 dc, ch 1, 2 dc) in same ch-space.
**Picot Shell** (3 dc, ch 3, slip st in top of dc at base of ch, 3 dc) in same ch-space.

### YOKE BACK

Leaving short tail for joining, ch 37 (43, 49). Work Row 1 into the nub in the back of the ch.
**Row 1 (WS)** Dc in 4th ch from hook and in each ch across; turn—35 (41, 47) dc.
**Note** Begin working dc through the back loop only, except last dc of row as specified.
**Row 2** Ch 3, skip first and 2nd dc, dc in next dc, cross behind and dc in first dc. Work 15 (18, 21) more Crosses, skip next dc, dc through both loops of t-ch; turn—16 (19, 22) Crosses.
**Row 3** Ch 3, skip first dc, dc in each dc to end, dc through both loops of t-ch; turn—35 (41, 47) dc.
**SIZE NEWBORN**
**Rows 4–6** Repeat Rows 2–3 once, then Row 2 once more.
**SIZE 6 MONTHS**
**Rows 4–7** Repeat Rows 2–3 twice.

**SIZE 12 MONTHS**

**Rows 4–8** Repeat Rows 2–3 twice, then Row 2 once more.

**SIZE NEWBORN**

**Row 1** Ch 3, skip first dc, dc in next 10 dc, dc through both loops of next dc; turn—12 dc. Leave remaining sts unworked.

**Row 2** Ch 3, work 5 Crosses, dc through both loops of t-ch; turn.

**SIZE 6 MONTHS**

**Row 1** Ch 3, work 6 Crosses, skip next dc, dc through both loops of next dc; turn. Leave remaining sts unworked.

**SIZE 12 MONTHS**

**Row 1** Ch 3, skip first dc, dc in next 14 dc, dc through both loops of next dc; turn—16 dc. Leave remaining sts unworked.

**Row 2** Ch 3, work 7 Crosses, dc through both loops of t-ch; turn.

**ALL SIZES**

**Row 1** Ch 3, skip first dc, dc in next 10 (12, 14) dc, 3 (1, 3) dc through both loops of next dc or t-ch; turn—14 (14, 18) dc.

**Row 2** Ch 3, work 6 (6, 8) Crosses, dc through both loops of t-ch; turn.

**Row 3** Ch 3, 0 (2, 0) dc in first dc, dc in next 12 (12, 16) dc, 3 (1, 3) dc through both loops of t-ch; turn—16 (16, 20) dc.

**Row 4** Ch 3, work 7 (7, 9) Crosses, dc through both loops of t-ch; turn.

**Row 5** Ch 3, 0 (2, 0) dc in first dc, dc in next 14 (14, 18) dc, 2 (1, 3) dc through both loops of t-ch; turn—17 (18, 22) dc.

**Row 6** Ch 3, work 7 (8, 10) Crosses, skip 1 (0, 0) st, dc in next 1 (0, 0) st, dc through both loops of t-ch; turn.

**SIZE NEWBORN**

Fasten off.

**SIZE 6 MONTHS**

**Row 7** Ch 3, 2 dc in first dc, dc in next 16 dc, dc through both loops of t-ch; turn—20 dc.

**Row 8** Ch 3, work 9 Crosses, dc through both loops of t-ch. Fasten off.

**SIZE 12 MONTHS**

**Row 7** Ch 3, skip first dc, dc in next 20 dc, 2 dc through both loops of t-ch; turn—23 dc.

**Row 8** Ch 3, work 10 Crosses, skip next st, dc in next st, dc through both loops of t-ch. Fasten off.

**ALL SIZES**

For other side of Front, skip next 11 (13, 15) unworked sts for neck; join in next st.

**SIZE 6 MONTHS**

**Row 1** Ch 3, work 6 Crosses, dc through both loops of t-ch; turn.

**ALL SIZES**

**Row 1** Ch 3, skip first dc, dc in next 10 (12, 14) dc, dc through both loops of t-ch; turn—12 (14, 16) dc.

**Row 2** Ch 3, work 5 (6, 7) Crosses, dc through both loops of t-ch; turn.

**Row 3** Ch 3, 2 (0, 2) dc in first dc, dc in next 10 (12, 14) dc, 1 (3, 1) dc through both loops of t-ch; turn—14 (16, 18) dc.

**Row 4** Ch 3, work 6 (7, 8) Crosses, dc through both loops of t-ch; turn.

**Row 5** Ch 3, 2 (0, 2) dc in first dc, dc in next 12 (14, 16) dc, 1 (3, 1) dc through both loops of t-ch; turn—16 (18, 20) dc.

**Row 6** Ch 3, work 7 (8, 9) Crosses, dc through both loops of t-ch; turn.

**Row 7** Ch 3, 1 (0, 2) dc in first dc, dc in next 14 (16, 18) dc, 1 (3, 1) dc through both loops of t-ch; turn—17 (20, 22) dc.

## SIZE NEWBORN

**Row 8** Ch 3, skip first dc, dc in next dc, work 7 Crosses, dc through both loops of t-ch.

## SIZE 6 MONTHS

**Row 8** Ch 3, work 9 Crosses, dc through both loops of t-ch.

## SIZE 12 MONTHS

**Row 8** Ch 3, work 10 Crosses, dc through both loops of t-ch; turn.

**Row 9** Ch 3, dc in first dc, dc in next 20 dc, dc through both loops of t-ch; turn—23 dc.

**Row 10** Ch 3, skip first dc, dc in next dc, work 10 Crosses, dc through both loops of t-ch.

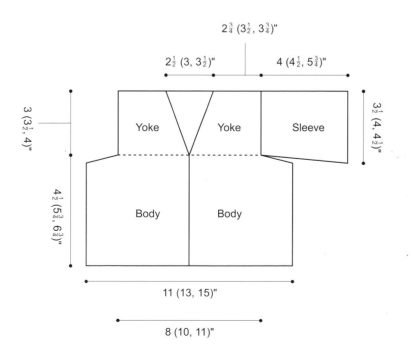

Join at underarm with slip stitch in spare loop of base ch at beg of Back. Fasten off. Join at other underarm with slip stitch using beg tail in adjacent st of Front. Fasten off.

### BODY

With WS facing, join to first dc at Front edge.

**Row 1** Ch 1, sc in first dc, sc in next dc, (ch 1, skip next dc, sc in next 2 dc) across; turn.

**Row 2** Ch 3, Shell in each ch-space across, dc in last sc; turn—22 (26, 30) Shells.

**Row 3** Ch 3, Shell in ch-space of each Shell across, dc in top of t-ch; turn.

Repeat last row 6 (8, 10) times—8 (10, 12) Shell rows total.

**Edging** With RS facing, ch 3, Picot Shell in ch-space of each Shell, dc in top of t-ch; work 2 sc in edge of each dc row up Right Front edge, sc in edge of sc row just before Yoke, 2 sc in edge of each dc row of V-neck, sc in each unworked st of neck, work sc in same manner down Left Front, slip stitch in top of last dc row edge. Fasten off.

**Row 2** With RS facing, join yarn at lower Right Front edge. Ch 3, dc in same st as joining, skip 2 sc, slip stitch in next sc, (ch 3, dc in same st as slip st, skip 2 sc, slip stitch in next sc) along Right Front, neck, and Left Front. Fasten off.

### SLEEVES

At underarm, with RS facing, join with slip stitch in edge of dc row of Yoke.

**Round 1** Ch 3, dc in edge of same row, [skip edge of next dc row, Shell in edge of next dc row] 6 (7, 8) times, 2 dc in edge of same row as beg, sc in top of beg ch; turn—7 (8, 9) Shells.

**Round 2** Slip stitch in first space, ch 3, dc in same space, Shell in ch-space of each Shell, 2 dc in same space as beg, sc in top of beg ch; turn. Repeat last round 5 (6, 8) times—7 (8, 10) Shell rows total.

**Edging** With RS facing, slip stitch in first space, ch 3, 2 dc in same space, Picot Shell in ch-space of each Shell, 3 dc in same space as beg, ch 3, slip stitch in top of dc at base of ch, slip stitch in top of beg ch. Fasten off.

### SELF BOW TIES—MAKE 2

Ch 69, sc in 2nd ch from hook, sc in next 3 ch, hdc in next ch, dc in next 2 ch, tr in next 20 ch, dc in next 2 ch, hdc in next ch, sc in next 37 ch, 3 sc in last ch. Working in spare loops of beg ch, sc in 37 loops, hdc in next loop, dc in next 2 loops, tr in next 20 loops, dc in next 2 loops, hdc in next loop, sc in last 4 loops. Fasten off, leaving a tail for sewing. Use tail to attach Tie to Front at base of V-neck.

RIBBON TIES (OPTIONAL)
Cut 1 yard (1 m) of ribbon in half. Turn under one raw edge on each piece and stitch a narrow hem. Sew other end to Front at base of V-neck.

# The First Fur

Originally intended as a christening shawl, this plush blanket will be the envy of everyone in the park. We kept the pretty stitch pattern faithful to the original design, but trimmed the edges with Fun Fur yarn. The look can be playful or posh. Opt for an all-white or cream palette for a baptism or naming ceremony, or lighten things up a little by picking a bright shade for the body of the blanket.

CROCHET **EASY**

SIZE

36" x 36" (91.5 x 91.5 cm)

MATERIALS

Ⓢ LION BRAND Homespun
*98% Acrylic, 2% Polyester*
*6 oz (170 g) 184 yd (169 m) Ball*
- 6 skeins #372 Sunshine State (A)
  or color of your choice

Ⓢ LION BRAND Fun Fur
*1³/₄ oz (50 g) 64 yd (58 m) Ball*
*100% Polyester*
- 3 balls #100 White (B)
  or color of your choice
- Size K-10.5 (6.5 mm) crochet hook
  OR SIZE TO OBTAIN GAUGE

GAUGE

2 pattern repeats = 5" (12.5 cm) with A.
BE SURE TO CHECK YOUR GAUGE.

## BLANKET

With A, ch 106.

**Foundation Row** 2 dc in 4th ch from hook, *ch 3, skip 3 ch, sc in next ch, skip 2 ch, 3 dc in next ch; repeat from * across, ending ch 3, skip 3 ch, sc in last ch; turn.

**Pattern Row** Ch 3, 2 dc in first sc, *ch 3, sc in next ch-3 space, skip 3 dc, 3 dc in next sc; repeat from * across, ending ch 3, sc in top of beg ch-3. Repeat Pattern Row until Blanket is a perfect square. Fasten off.

## FINISHING

With RS facing and 2 strands of B held tog, join yarn at upper right corner.

**Round 1** Ch 1, work sc in each sc around, working 3 sc in each corner; join with slip stitch to top of beg sc.

**Round 2** Ch 2, work hdc in each sc around, working 3 hdc in corner sc; join with slip stitch to top of beg hdc. Fasten off. Weave in ends.

# CHAPTER 7

# Fingers and Toes: Mittens, Gloves, Slippers, and Socks

Slipping your fingers into a pair of warm wool mittens is the next best thing to cupping a mug of piping hot cocoa between your palms. It's good old-fashioned comfort. Ditto for socks and slippers: there's something about padding around the house in a colorful pair that just makes the outside world go away.

Quick projects that make great gifts, slippers, socks, gloves, and mittens have always been popular with knitters and crocheters, and for that reason, ideas and instructions for making them are plentiful. That made our job of pulling together the patterns for this chapter at once very easy, yet exceedingly difficult—easy because there were so many to choose from, and hard, well, because there were so many to choose from!

# The Knit Wristlet

Yesteryear's simple, striped wristlets were meant for outdoor wear. Today's versions are a fun and fashionable way to keep your hands warm while clicking away—either at the computer keyboard or with knitting needles. Knit in chunky yarn, they're a perfect first-time project.

## KNIT EASY

### SIZE

**Circumference** 8″ (20.5 cm)

**Length** 8¹⁄₂″ (21.5 cm)

### MATERIALS

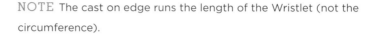

[5] LION BRAND Color Waves

*3 oz (85 g) 125 yd (113 m) Skein*

*83% Acrylic 17% Polyester*

- 1 skein #350 Night Sky or color of your choice
- Size 10 (6 mm) knitting needles OR SIZE TO OBTAIN GAUGE
- Size 10 (6 mm) double-pointed needles
- Large-eyed, blunt needle

### GAUGE

12 sts + 24 rows = 4″ (10 cm) in Garter Stitch (knit every row).

BE SURE TO CHECK YOUR GAUGE.

**NOTE** The cast on edge runs the length of the Wristlet (not the circumference).

### WRISTLET

Cast on 25 sts. Work even in Garter Stitch until piece measures 8″ (20.5 cm) or desired circumference. Bind off.

### FINISHING

With WS facing and double-pointed needle, pick up and knit one st in each ridge along selvage edge. Cast on 3 sts and work i-cord bind-off (see Techniques, page 188) along edge. Repeat for second selvage edge. Sew cast-on edge to bind-off edge for 2″ (5 cm). Leave a 1¹⁄₂″ (4 cm) opening for thumb, then sew remaining 4¹⁄₂″ (11.5 cm) of cast-on edge to bind off edge. Weave in ends.

# The Crocheted Wristlet

Wristlets of old were utilitarian accessories made in simple yarns and uninspired colors. Today, just grab your favorite novelty yarn and whip up a pair or two (or three or four) of these beginner-friendly wrist warmers. Fast and fun to make, they make great gifts and great fashion statements. Plus, they keep your fingers free for digging out subway tokens—or crocheting another pair.

CROCHET **EASY**

## SIZE

**Circumference** 8″ (20.5 cm)

**Length** 8″ (20.5 cm)

## MATERIALS

LION BRAND Fancy Fur

*1³/₄ oz (50 g) 39 yd (35 m) Ball*

*55% Polyamide, 45% Polyester*

- 2 balls #213 Rainbow Red
  or color of your choice
- Size P-15 (10 mm) crochet hook
  OR SIZE TO OBTAIN GAUGE

## GAUGE

6 sc + 7 rounds = 4″ (10 cm).
BE SURE TO CHECK YOUR GAUGE.

## WRISTLET

Ch 12; join with slip stitch to form ring.

**Round 1** Ch 1, sc in each ch around; join with slip stitch to beg sc—12 sc.

**Round 2** Ch 1, sc in each sc around; join with slip stitch to beg sc.

Repeat Round 2 until piece measures 5¹/₂″ (14 cm), or desired length to thumb opening.

**Thumb opening** Ch 1, sc in first sc, ch 3, skip 3 sc, sc in each sc around; join with slip stitch to beg sc.

**Next round** Ch 1, sc in each sc and ch around; join with slip stitch to beg sc—12 sc.

Work even in sc until piece measures 8″ (20.5 cm) or desired length. Fasten off. Weave in ends.

# The Gauntlet

A super-easy pattern deserves to be worked over and over again. Try making these wrist warmers with thumb openings in a variety of yarns—fur, boucle, chunkies, or anything else that strikes your fancy.

CROCHET **EASY**

SIZE

**Circumference** 8" (20.5 cm)

**Length** 8" (20.5 cm)

MATERIALS

**(4)** LION BRAND Glitterspun

*1³/₄ oz (50 g) 115 yd (105 m) Ball*

*60% Acrylic, 27% Cupro, 13% Polyester*

- 2 balls #135 Bronze
  or color of your choice

**(5)** LION BRAND Fun Fur

*1³/₄ oz (50 g) 64 yd (58 m) Ball*

*100% Polyester*

- 3 balls #132 Olive
  or color of your choice

- Size N-13 (9 mm) crochet hook OR
  SIZE TO OBTAIN GAUGE

GAUGE

8 sc + 10 rounds = 4" (10 cm) with 1 strand each of Glitterspun and Fun Fur held tog.

BE SURE TO CHECK YOUR GAUGE.

WRISTLET

With 1 strand each of Glitterspun and Fun Fur held tog, ch 16; join with slip stitch to form ring.

**Round 1** Ch 1, sc in each ch around; join with slip stitch to beg sc—16 sc.

**Round 2** Ch 1, sc in each sc around; join with slip stitch to beg sc.

Repeat Round 2 until piece measures 5¹/₂" (14 cm), or desired length to thumb opening.

**Thumb opening** Ch 1, sc in first sc, ch 4, skip 4 sc, sc in each sc around; join with slip stitch to beg sc.

**Next round** Ch 1, sc in each sc and ch around; join with slip stitch to beg sc—16 sc.

Work even in sc until piece measures 8" (20.5 cm) or desired length. Fasten off. Weave in ends.

# Bright Striped Mittens

We took a pattern for a prim, elbow-length evening mitten and scaled it down for everyday. Made in a self-striping yarn (just start knitting and the stripe pattern appears like magic), they'll be a bright spot in a bleak winter day.

KNIT **INTERMEDIATE**

## SIZE

To fit average woman's hand
**Circumference** 7 1/2" (19 cm)

## MATERIALS

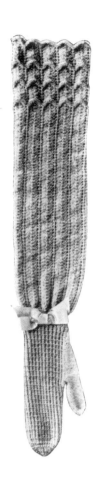

(2) LION BRAND Magic Stripes
*3 1/2 oz (100 g) 330 yd (300 m) Ball*
*75% Superwash Wool, 25% Nylon*

- 2 balls #200 Jelly Bean Stripe or color of your choice
- Size 3 (3.25 mm) double-pointed needles (set of 4) OR SIZE TO OBTAIN GAUGE
- Stitch markers
- Small amount of waste yarn
- Large-eyed, blunt needle

## GAUGE

28 sts + 42 rounds = 4" (10 cm) in Chevron Pattern.
40 sts + 38 rounds = 4" (10 cm) in K 1, P 1 Rib.
BE SURE TO CHECK YOUR GAUGE.

## STITCH EXPLANATION

**Sk2p** Slip 1 as if to knit, k2tog, pass the slipped stitch over the k2tog stitch.

## PATTERN STITCH

**CHEVRON PATTERN (multiple of 10 stitches)**
**Rounds 1–3** Purl.
**Round 4** *Knit 1, yarn over, knit 3, sk2p, knit 3, yarn over; repeat from *.
**Round 5** Knit.
**Rounds 7–12** Repeat Rounds 4 and 5 three more times.
Repeat Rounds 1–12 for Chevron Pattern.

## LEFT MITTEN

Cast on 50 sts. For ease of working pattern, place 20 sts on the first 2 needles and 10 sts on the third one. Join and place marker for beg of round.

**Cuff** Work 2 repeats of Chevron Pattern, then work Rounds 1–10.

**Next round** *K 2, M1 (see Techniques, page 188); repeat from * around—75 sts.

**Hand** Beg K 1, P 1 Rib and inc 1 st on round—76 sts. Redistribute stitches so that there are 24 on the first needle and 26 on each of the next two needles. Work in rib for 1" (2.5 cm).

**Thumb gusset** Rib to last 3 sts of round, place marker, M1L (see Techniques, page 188), k 1, M1R (see Techniques, page 188), place marker, rib to end of round.

**Next round** Rib to marker, slip marker, k to next marker, slip marker, rib to end of round.

**Inc Round** Rib to marker, slip marker, M1L, k to next marker, M1R, slip marker, rib to end of round.

Repeat Inc Round every 2nd round 3 more times, then every 3rd round 4 times until there are 19 sts between markers—94 sts. Work 4 rounds even.

**Next round** Work in rib to marker, put 19 thumb sts on waste yarn and tie in loop to hold, remove gusset markers, cast on 5 sts, rib to end—80 sts. Continue in rib as established until Mitten measures 5" (12.5 cm) from beg of hand, or desired length to top of little finger.

**Next round** *Rib 2, ssk (see Techniques, page 188), rib 32, k2tog, place marker, rib 2; repeat from *—76 sts.

**Dec Round** *Rib 2, ssk, rib to 2 sts before marker, k2tog, rib 2; repeat from *—72 sts.

Work Dec Round every round 13 more times—20 sts.

**Next round** *Rib 2, ssk, k2tog, k2tog, rib 2; repeat from *—14 sts.

Break yarn, leaving a 5" (12.5 cm) tail. Using large-eyed, blunt needle, draw tail through remaining sts 2 times, gathering them together. Anchor tail on inside of mitten.

**Finish thumb** Place 19 sts from waste yarn onto 2 needles; with a 3rd needle, pick up and k 5 sts in cast on sts—24 sts. Join and k each round until thumb measures about 1 1/2" (4 cm), or desired length to mid-thumbnail.

**Dec Round** *K 2, k2tog; repeat from *—18 sts. Work 1 round even.

**Dec Round** *K 1, k2tog; repeat from *—12 sts.

**Dec Round** K2tog around—6 sts.

Using large-eyed, blunt needle, draw tail through remaining sts 2 times, gathering them together. Anchor tail on inside of mitten.

RIGHT MITTEN

Work as for Left Mitten to thumb gusset.

**Thumb gusset** Rib 3, place marker, M1L, k 1, M1R, place marker, rib to end of round.

Continue to work thumb gusset as established. Finish as for Left Mitten.

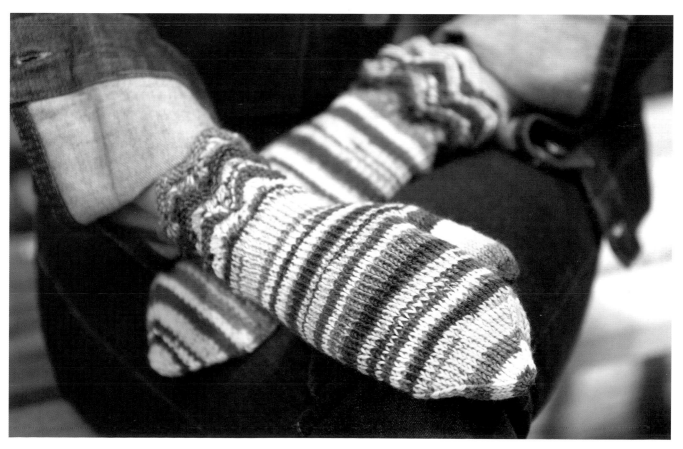

# Striped Gloves

How do you make a glove grand? Start with a tried-and-true pattern and then update it in a self-striping yarn. The result is a bold-banded pattern that works up effortlessly without the need to constantly change colors. This simple change sets our funky pair apart from the purely functional original.

## KNIT **INTERMEDIATE**

### SIZE

To fit average man's hand

**Circumference** 8″ (20.5 cm)

### MATERIALS

**2** LION BRAND Magic Stripes

*3¹/₂ oz (100 g) 330 yd (300 m) Ball*

*75% Superwash Wool, 25% Nylon*

- 1 ball #205 Brown/Blue
  or color of your choice
- Size 3 (3.25 mm) double-pointed
  needles (set of 4) OR SIZE TO
  OBTAIN GAUGE
- Size 2 (2.75 mm) double-pointed
  needles (set of 4)
- Stitch markers
- Small amount of waste yarn
- Large-eyed, blunt needle

### GAUGE

28 sts + 37 rows = 4″ (10 cm) in Pattern Stitch on larger needles.

BE SURE TO CHECK YOUR GAUGE.

### PATTERN STITCH (multiple of 2 sts)

**Rounds 1 and 2** Knit.

**Round 3** *K 1, p 1; repeat from *.

Repeat Rounds 1–3 for Pattern Stitch.

### LEFT GLOVE

With larger needles, cast on 56 sts loosely. Place 20 sts on first two needles and 16 sts on third needle. Join and place marker for beg of round. **Cuff** Purl 1 round. Change to smaller needles and work in K 2, P 2 Rib for 2¹/₂″ (6.5 cm). Change to larger needles and work 5 rounds in Pattern Stitch.

**Thumb gusset** Slip marker, M1L (see Techniques, page 188), k 1, M1R (see Techniques, page 188), place marker, work in Pattern Stitch to end of round—58 sts. Work 3 rounds even.

**Inc Round** Slip marker, M1L, work in Pattern Stitch to next marker, M1R, slip marker, work to end of round.

Repeat Inc Round every 4th round until there are 17 sts between markers—72 sts. Work 5 rounds even. Place 17 thumb sts onto waste yarn and tie in loop. Remove markers.

**Next round** Cast on 3 sts to replace thumb sts, place marker for beg of round—58 sts. Work even until Glove measures 4¹/₄″ (11 cm) from end of ribbing, or desired length to base of fingers.

**Index finger** Knit 9; slip all sts except last 7 onto waste yarn; use a 3rd needle and cast on 4 sts for the inside of the finger—20 sts.

Redistribute sts on 3 needles and work in Pattern Stitch for 3″ (7.5 cm), or ¹/₂″ (1.5 cm) less than desired length.

**Dec Round 1** *K 3, k2tog; repeat from *—16 sts.

Work 2 rounds even.

**Dec Round 2** *K 2, k2tog; repeat from *—12 sts.

Work 1 round even.

**Dec Round 3** *K 1, k2tog; repeat from *—8 sts.

Draw yarn through remaining sts, pull tight and fasten yarn firmly on WS.

**Middle finger** Slip the first 7 sts from waste yarn onto a needle. Cast on 3 sts onto another needle. Slip the last 7 sts from waste yarn and place on a third needle, then pick up and knit 3 sts where the 4 were cast on for Index Finger—20 sts. Redistribute sts on needles as necessary. Work in Pattern Stitch for 3 1/4" (8.5 cm), or 1/2" (1.5 cm) less than desired length. Dec and finish as for Index Finger.

**Ring finger** Slip the next 7 sts from waste yarn onto a needle, cast on 3 sts, slip the last 7 sts from waste yarn onto a needle, pick up and knit 3 sts from cast on sts of Middle Finger—20 sts. Redistribute sts on needles as necessary. Work in Pattern Stitch for 3 1/8" (8 cm), or 1/2" (1.5 cm) less than desired length, then dec and finish as for Pointer Finger.

**Little finger** Slip the remaining 14 sts from waste yarn onto 2 needles, then pick up and knit 2 sts from the cast-on sts of Ring Finger—16 sts. Redistribute sts on needles as necessary. Work in Pattern Stitch for $2^1/4$" (5.5 cm), or $1/4$" (0.5 cm) less than desired length.

**Dec Round 1** *K 2, k2tog; repeat from *, ending k 2—11 sts.

Work 1 round even.

**Dec Round 2** *K 1, k2tog; repeat from *, ending k 2—8 sts.

Draw yarn through remaining sts, pull tight, and fasten yarn firmly on WS.

**Finish thumb** Slip the 17 sts from waste yarn onto 2 needles, then pick up and knit 3 sts from the cast-on sts of Hand. Redistribute sts on needles as necessary. Work in Pattern Stitch for $2^3/4$" (7 cm), or $1/2$" (1.5 cm) less than desired length.

**Dec Round 1** *K 3, k2tog; repeat from *, ending k 2—14 sts.

Work 2 rounds even.

**Dec Round 2** *K 2, k2tog; repeat from *, ending k 2—11 sts.

Work 1 round even.

**Dec Round 3** *K 1, k2tog; repeat from *, ending k 2—8 sts.

Draw yarn through remaining sts, pull tight, and fasten yarn firmly on WS.

Weave in ends.

## RIGHT GLOVE

Work as for Left Glove until thumb sts are on waste yarn.

**Next round** Place marker for beg of round, cast on 3 sts, work in Pattern Stitch to end of round.

Finish as for Left Glove.

# In-a-Jiffy Hat and Mittens

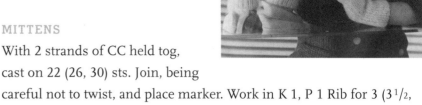

We made fast work of this cozy hat and mitten set (circa 1950s) by knitting it in a soft and chunky yarn. Faux fur trim at the brim and cuffs glam things up a little, but the pattern is simple enough for a beginner to tackle—with great results.

KNIT **EASY**

### SIZE

Mittens S (M, L)

**Circumference** 6¹/₂ (7¹/₂, 8¹/₂)" [16.5 (19, 21.5) cm]

**Hat** S/M (L)

**Circumference** 21¹/₄ (23¹/₂)" [54 (59.5) cm]

**Note** Before beginning pattern, circle all numbers pertaining to your size for ease in working.

### MATERIALS

🔵⑤ LION BRAND Jiffy

2¹/₂ oz (70 g) 115 yd (103 m) Ball
100% Acrylic

- 2 balls #307 Denver Print (MC)
  or color of your choice

🔵⑤ LION BRAND Fun Fur

1³/₄ oz (50 g) 64 yd (58 m) Ball
100% Polyester

- 3 balls #109 Sapphire (CC)
  or color of your choice
- Size 10 (6 mm) double-pointed
  needles OR SIZE TO OBTAIN
  GAUGE
- Stitch markers
- Stitch holder
- Large-eyed, blunt needle

### GAUGE

15 sts + 24 rounds = 4" (10 cm) in Stockinette stitch (knit every round) with MC.

BE SURE TO CHECK YOUR GAUGE.

### MITTENS

With 2 strands of CC held tog, cast on 22 (26, 30) sts. Join, being careful not to twist, and place marker. Work in K 1, P 1 Rib for 3 (3¹/₂, 4)" [7.5 (9, 10) cm], inc one st on last round—23 (27, 31) sts. Change to 1 strand of MC and work in St st for 4 (5, 6) rounds.

**Shape thumb gusset** M1L (see Techniques, page 188), k 1, M1R (see Techniques, page 188), place marker, k to end of round—25 (29, 33) sts. Work 3 rounds in St st.

**Next round** M1L, k 3, M1R, slip marker, k to end of round—27 (31, 35) sts.

Inc after first marker and before second marker every 4th round 2 (2, 3) more times—31 (35, 41) sts.

**Next round** K 9 (9, 11) sts and place these sts on holder. Cast on 2 sts at beg of needle, k to end of round and join—24 (28, 32) sts. Continue to work even in St st until Mitten measures 7 (7¹/₂, 8)" [18 (19, 20.5) cm] from cuff, or until ¹/₂" (1.5 cm) less than desired length.

**Next round** *K 2, k2tog, repeat from *—18 (21, 24) sts.

**Next round** *K 1, k2tog, repeat from *—12 (14, 16) sts.

**Next round** K2tog around—6 (7, 8) sts.

Cut yarn and, with needle, run yarn through remaining sts and pull to fasten.

**Finish Thumb** With RS facing and MC, pick up and k 3 sts along cast-on edge and k across thumb sts on holder—12 (12, 14) sts. Work even in St st until Thumb measures 3" (7.5 cm), or desired length.

**Next round** K2tog around—6 (6, 7) sts.

Cut yarn and, with needle, run yarn through remaining sts and pull to fasten. Weave in ends.

With 2 strands of CC held tog, cast on 80 (88) sts. Join, being careful not to twist, and place marker. Work in K 1, P 1 Rib for 4 (4 1/2)" [10 (11.5) cm]. Change to 1 strand of MC and work in St st for 4 (4 1/2)" [10 (11.5) cm].

**Next round** *K 6, k2tog, repeat from *—70 (77) sts.

**Next round** *K 5, k2tog, repeat from *—60 (66) sts.

Continue to dec as established (working 1 fewer k st before k2tog) until 10 (11) sts remain.

**Next round** K2tog around, ending k2tog (k3tog)—5 sts.

Cut yarn and, with needle, run yarn through remaining sts and pull to fasten. Weave in ends. Turn up brim of Hat.

# Red-Hot Slippers

Forget walking! These boots were made for lounging. Slip them on before you stumble out of bed on a Saturday morning and keep them on all day. The originals were made on small needles in a combination of pink and blue, but we knit them in a shocking shade of red to really wake things up.

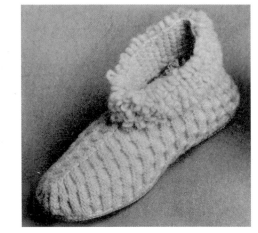

KNIT **EASY**

## SIZE

Woman's shoe size 5–6 (7–8, 9–10, 11–12)

**Length** 8 (9, 10, 11)" [20.5 (23, 25.5, 28) cm]

**Note** Before beginning pattern, circle all numbers pertaining to your size for ease in working.

## MATERIALS

(4) LION BRAND Wool-Ease

*3 oz (85 g) 197 yd (180 m) Ball*

*80% Acrylic, 20% Wool*

- 2 (2, 3, 3) balls #102 Ranch Red or color of your choice
- Size 8 (5 mm) knitting needles OR SIZE TO OBTAIN GAUGE
- Stitch holders
- Stitch markers
- Large-eyed, blunt needle

## GAUGE

22 sts + 44 rows = 4" (10 cm) in Basket Pattern Stitch with one strand of yarn. BE SURE TO CHECK YOUR GAUGE.

NOTE Work all decreases in pattern.

## PATTERN STITCHES

**BASKET PATTERN STITCH (multiple of 6 sts + 4)**

**Row 1 (RS)** Knit.

**Row 2** Purl.

**Rows 3 and 5** K 1, *slip 2 with yarn in back, k 4; repeat from *, ending slip 2, k 1.

**Rows 4 and 6** K 1, *slip 2 with yarn in front, k 4; repeat from *, ending slip 2, k 1.

**Row 7** Knit.

**Row 8** Purl.

**Rows 9 and 11** K 4, *slip 2 with yarn in back, k 4; repeat from *.

**Rows 10 and 12** K 4, *slip 2 with yarn in front, k 4; repeat from *.

Repeat Rows 1–12 for Basket Pattern Stitch.

**DOUBLE GARTER STITCH**

**Row 1 (WS)** Knit.

**Rows 2 and 3** Purl.

**Row 4** Knit.

Repeat Rows 1–4 for Double Garter Stitch.

**LOOP PATTERN STITCH**

**Row 1 (RS)** *Knit into st, keeping st on left needle. Bring yarn forward and wrap around left thumb, bring yarn back and knit same st as before, this time slipping st from left needle. Yarn over, pass both sts on right needle over this yarn over; repeat from * in each st across row.

**Row 2** Knit.

Repeat Rows 1–2 for Loop Pattern Stitch.

**SIDE BACK—MAKE 2 FOR EACH SLIPPER**

With single strand of yarn, cast on 16 (16, 22, 22) sts. Work 3 (3, 4, 4) repeats of Basket Pattern Stitch. Place sts on holder or spare needle. Make second piece as for first.

**Join side back pieces** With RS facing, knit across piece to last 3 sts, k2tog, knit last st of first piece tog with first st of second piece, k2tog, k to end—29 (29, 41, 41) sts.

**Next row** Purl 13 (13, 19, 19) sts, place marker, p 3, place marker, p remaining 13 (13, 19, 19) sts.

**Next row (RS)** Work Row 3 of Basket Pattern Stitch to marker, k 1, slip 1, k 1, work Row 3 of pattern to end.

Continue to work in pattern as established, working center 3 sts as k 1, slip 1, k 1 on RS and p 3 on WS and, AT THE SAME TIME, dec one st before first marker and after second marker on Rows 1 and 7, until Slipper measures 7 (8, 9, 10)" [18 (20.5, 23, 25.5) cm] from beg or 1" (2.5 cm) less than desired length. Then, while maintaining pattern, dec one st before first marker and after second marker every RS row 4 times.

**Next row** K2tog across row, ending k 1. Bind off.

## SOLE

With RS facing and single strand of yarn, pick up and knit 32 (36, 40, 44) sts along right side of Slipper, 6 (6, 8, 8) sts along Front, and 32 (36, 40, 44) sts along left side of Slipper—70 (78, 88, 96) sts.

**Next row (WS)** Join 2nd strand of yarn. With 2 strands of yarn held tog, k 3 (3, 4, 4), place marker, k 29 (33, 36, 40), place marker, k 6 (6, 8, 8), place marker, k 29 (33, 36, 40), place marker, k 3 (3, 4, 4).

**Next row** Work Row 2 of Double Garter Stitch.

Continue to work in Double Garter Stitch, working Row 4 as follows: *K to 2 sts before marker, k2tog, work to next marker, slip marker, ssk (see Techniques, page 188); repeat from * once more. Continue to work in pattern, dec on Row 4 until 2 sts remain between 2 center markers—62 (70, 76, 84) sts. Work 4 more rows in Double Garter Stitch. Bind off.

## FINISHING

With single strand of yarn, cast on 34 (34, 40, 40) sts using long tail cast-on. Work 7 rows of Loop Pattern Stitch. Bind off. Sew bound off edge to top of Slipper opening. Sew sole and back Slipper seams. Weave in ends.

# The Sandal Sock

Grandma may have stitched up socks like this for your dad to keep his feet warm inside his winter boots, but knit in a swirl of colorful stripes, these cozy footwarmers are made to be seen. Perfect for pairing with your favorite Birkenstocks or just padding around the house, this reinterpretation of the classic trouser sock only looks complicated—the cool colorwork pattern is created with self-striping yarn.

KNIT **INTERMEDIATE**

## SIZE

**Leg circumference** 10″ (25.5 cm)

**Foot circumference** 8 1/2″ (21.5 cm)

**Leg length** 13 1/2″ (34.5 cm)

## MATERIALS

**2** LION BRAND Magic Stripes

*3 1/2 oz (100 g) 330 yd (300 m) Ball*

*75% Superwash Wool, 25% Nylon*

- 2 balls #206 Lumberjack Black Pattern
  or color of your choice
- Size 1 (2.25 mm) and size 2 (2.75 mm) double-pointed needles (set of 5) OR SIZE TO OBTAIN GAUGE
- Large-eyed, blunt needle

## GAUGE

30 sts + 40 rounds = 4″ (10 cm) in Stockinette stitch (knit every round) on larger needles.

BE SURE TO CHECK YOUR GAUGE.

NOTE Slip all stitches as if to purl.

## STITCH EXPLANATION

**Grafting Stockinette stitch (aka weaving stitches together, Kitchener St)** Leave stitches to be grafted on needles and place wrong sides of fabric together with needles pointing to the right. Cut the yarn, leaving a tail about 3 times the length of the edge to be grafted. Thread yarn onto a blunt needle.

### SET UP

**a)** Slip sewing needle purlwise into the first st of the *front* knitting needle and pull the yarn through. Do not drop the st off the knitting needle.

**b)** Slip sewing needle knitwise into the first st of the *back* knitting needle knitways and pull through. Do not drop the st off the knitting needle.

### Step 1. FRONT NEEDLE

Using one motion, slip sewing needle **knitwise** through the first st on the front knitting needle and **let it drop** from the needle; next, slip sewing needle **purlwise** into next st on front needle and pull yarn through. **Leave 2nd st on needle.**

### Step 1. BACK NEEDLE

Using one motion, slip sewing needle **purlwise** through the first st on the back needle and **let it drop** from the needle; next, slip the needle **knitwise** into the next st on the back needle and pull yarn through. **Leave 2nd st on needle.** Repeat Steps 1 & 2 until all stitches are grated together. [**Hint—repeat the words in bold** to yourself as you do this and you will get into a rhythm.]

### SOCKS

With larger needles, loosely cast on 76 sts. Arrange sts on 4 double-pointed needles as follows:

**Needle 1 (N1)** 22 heel sts.

**Needle 2 (N2)** 16 instep sts.

**Needle 3 (N3)** 16 instep sts.

**Needle 4 (N4)** 22 heel sts.

Join, being careful not to twist. P 1. Change to smaller needles and work in 2, 2 rib for 4¹/₂" (11.5 cm).

Change to larger needles. P 1 ("seam" st), knit to end of round. Work even until piece measures 7" (18 cm) from beg.

**Dec for ankle** P 1, k 1, k2tog, k to last 3 sts of N4, ssk (see Techniques, page 188), k 1.

Repeat dec rnd every 4th round 5 more times—64 sts (16 sts on each needle). Work even until piece measures 11" (28 cm) from beg.

### HEEL FLAP

Work sts on N1-N3, then slip sts from N4 onto N1—32 sts on N1.
Begin working back and forth on N1 (heel sts).

**Row 1** (RS) *Slip 1, k 1; repeat from * to end of row.

**Row 2** Slip 1, p to end of row.

Repeat these 2 rows until 32 rows are complete.

### TURN HEEL

**Row 1** (RS) K 17, ssk, k 1; turn.

**Row 2** Slip 1, p 3, p2tog, p 1; turn.

**Row 3** Slip 1, k 4, ssk, k 1; turn.

**Row 4** Slip 1, p 5, p2tog, p 1; turn.

**Row 5** Slip 1, k 6, ssk, k 1; turn.

**Row 6** Slip 1, p 7, p2tog, p 1; turn.

**Row 7** Slip 1, k 8, ssk, k 1; turn.

**Row 8** Slip 1, p 9, p2tog, p 1; turn.

**Row 9** Slip 1, k 10, ssk, k 1; turn.

**Row 10** Slip 1, p 11, p2tog, p 1; turn.

**Row 11** Slip 1, k 12, ssk, k 1; turn.

**Row 12** Slip 1, p 13, p2tog, p 1; turn.

**Row 13** Slip 1, k 14, ssk, k 1; turn.

**Row 14** Slip 1, p 15, p2tog, p 1; turn.

Knit 9 sts. This is now the beg of round.

## GUSSET

**N1** With free needle, k second half of heel sts. Continuing with same needle, pick up and knit 16 sts along left side of heel flap. Pick up and knit one st from the row below the first instep st to prevent a hole—26 sts.

**N2** With free needle, k 16 instep sts.

**N3** With free needle, k remaining 16 instep sts.

**N4** With free needle, pick up and knit one st from the row below the last instep st to prevent a hole. Pick up and k 16 sts along right side of heel flap. K remaining 9 heel sts—26 sts.

**Round 1** K to last 3 sts on N1, k2tog, k 1; k all sts on N2 and N3; on N4, k 1, ssk, k to end.

**Round 2** Knit.

Repeat Rounds 1–2 until 64 sts remain (16 sts on each needle).

## FOOT

Work even until foot measures 8 1/2" (21.5 cm), or 2" (5 cm) less than desired length to end of toe.

## TOE

**Round 1** K to last 3 sts on N1, k2tog, k 1; on N2, k 1, ssk, k to end; on N3, k to last 3 sts, k2tog, k 1; on N4, k 1, ssk, k to end.

**Round 2** K.

Repeat these 2 rounds until 32 sts remain (8 sts on each needle).

Work round 1 only until 16 sts remain (4 sts on each needle).

## FINISHING

Knit sts on N1. Slip sts from N4 onto N1.

Slip sts from N3 onto N2. Holding N1 and N2 together, graft sts (see stitch explanation, page 168). Weave in ends.

# CHAPTER 8

# The Home Front: Blankets, Throws, and More

Knitting or crocheting for the home is a surprisingly satisfying experience. A sweater, you see, isn't worn every day. But a blanket or throw tossed across a sofa or armchair with intent, now that's another story. You can admire it every time you walk by—and so can everyone else.

Vintage patterns for home projects are perhaps the most easily adaptable of the lot. Sizing is more or less irrelevant (have you ever tried on an afghan that didn't fit?) and there's usually no shaping involved. The primary revision that you will have to make is to gauge. Since most vintage afghans were knit with much thinner yarns, you must swatch the stitch pattern to decide whether you can work it in a much larger gauge, or whether you must modify the stitch in order to maintain the overall proportion.

# The Navajo Blanket

This desert beauty pays homage to the artful Native American weavings that continue to be popular souvenirs of the American Southwest. Equally at home in the den or a dorm room, the blanket looks great on both sides. We lightened the palette a little, and crocheted it in a soft wool blend for added comfort.

CROCHET **EASY+**

## SIZE
53" x 72" (134.5 x 183 cm)

## MATERIALS
LION BRAND Wool-Ease
*3 oz (85 g) 197 yd (180 m) Ball*
*80% Acrylic, 20% Wool*
- 14 balls #102 Ranch Red (A)
- 2 balls #152 Oxford Gray (B)
- 2 balls #099 Fisherman (C)
- 2 balls #153 Black (D)
- 2 balls #151 Gray Heather (E) or colors of your choice
- Size J-10 (6 mm) crochet hook OR SIZE TO OBTAIN GAUGE

## GAUGE
15 sc + 16 rows = 4" (10 cm).
BE SURE TO CHECK YOUR GAUGE.

NOTE Ch 1 at end of each row.

## AFGHAN

With A, ch 200. Sc in 2nd ch from hook and in each ch across; ch 1, turn—199 sc. Work 6 more rows sc.

Work the afghan chart (see page 176) 3 times across in sc as follows:

**Row 1** 11A, 45B, 21A, 45B, 21A, 45B, 11A.

**Row 2** 10A, 47B, 19A, 47B, 19A, 47B, 10A.

Break off B; join C.

**Row 3** 9A, 49C, 17A, 49C, 17A, 49C, 9A.

**Row 4** 8A, 51C, 15A, 51C, 15A, 51C, 8A.

Break off C; join D.

**Row 5** 18A, 31D, 35A, 31D, 35A, 31D, 18A.

**Row 6** 17A, 33D, 33A, 33D, 33A, 33D, 17A.

**Row 7** 16A, 35D, 31A, 35D, 31A, 35D, 16A.

Break off D; join C.

**Row 8** 19A, 29C, 37A, 29C, 37A, 29C, 19A.

**Row 9** 18A, 31C, 35A, 31C, 35A, 31C, 18A.

Break off C; join D.

**Row 10** 27A, 13D, 53A, 13D, 53A, 13D, 27A.

Break off D; join E.

**Row 11** 22A, 23E, 43A, 23E, 43A, 23E, 22A.

**Row 12** 21A, 25E, 41A, 25E, 41A, 25E, 21A.

**Row 13** 20A, 27E, 39A, 27E, 39A, 27E, 20A.

Break off E.

**Rows 14–17** With A, sc in each sc across.

Join D.

**Row 18** 6A, 10D, 35A, 10D, 11A, 10D, 35A, 10D, 11A, 10D, 35A, 10D, 6A.

Break off D; join C.

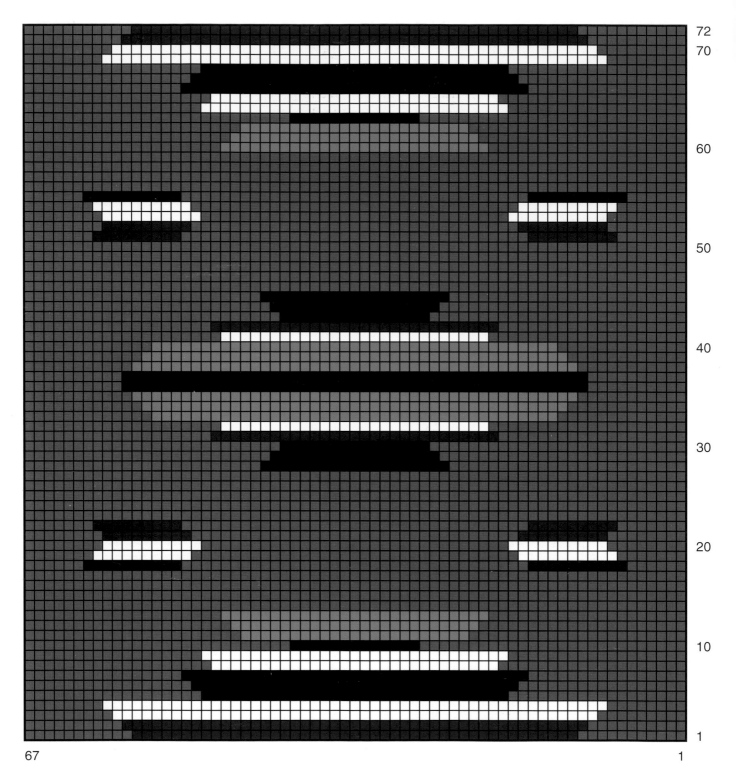

72
70

60

50

40

30

20

10

1

67

1

NOTE: Work sts 1–67, then (2–67) twice. Work Rows 1–72 a total of 4 times.

**Row 19** 7A, 10C, 33A, 10C, 13A, 10C, 33A, 10C, 13A, 10C, 33A, 10C, 7A.

**Row 20** 8A, 10C, 31A, 10C, 15A, 10C, 31A, 10C, 15A, 10C, 31A, 10C, 8A.

Break off C; join B.

**Row 21** 8A, 10B, 31A, 10B, 15A, 10B, 31A, 10B, 15A, 10B, 31A, 10B, 8A.

**Row 22** 7A, 10B, 33A, 10B, 13A, 10B, 33A, 10B, 13A, 10B, 33A, 10B, 7A.

Break off B.

**Rows 23–27** With A, sc in each sc across.

Join D.

**Row 28** 25A, 17D, 49A, 17D, 49A, 17D, 25A.

**Row 29** 26A, 15D, 51A, 15D, 51A, 15D, 26A.

**Row 30** 27A, 13D, 53A, 13D, 53A, 13D, 27A.

Break off D; join B.

**Row 31** 20A, 27B, 39A, 27B, 39A, 27B, 20A.

Break off B; join C.

**Row 32** 21A, 25C, 41A, 25C, 41A, 25C, 21A.

Break off C; join E.

**Row 33** 14A, 39E, 27A, 39E, 27A, 39E, 14A.

**Row 34** 13A, 41E, 25A, 41E, 25A, 41E, 13A.

**Row 35** 12A, 43E, 23A, 43E, 23A, 43E, 12A.

Break off E, join D.

**Row 36** 11A, 45D, 21A, 45D, 21A, 45D, 11A.

This completes one half of the pattern.

**Rows 37–72** Work as for rows 36–1.

Work Rows 1–72 three more times.

With A, work 7 rows sc. At end of last row, do not turn. Work 1 rnd sc evenly spaced along each edge of afghan, working 2 sc in each corner. Join with slip stitch to first corner sc. Fasten off. Weave in ends.

# The Understated Shaded Afghan

Afghans in graduated colors have been a favorite for decades. Soft, modulating stripes make this simple crochet coverlet look at home in any setting. We chose nature-inspired colors of our silky Homespun to create the soothing, painterly effect; you can easily recolor the palette to suit your décor. A scalloped border pulls it all together.

### SIZE

61" x 49" (155 x 124.5 cm), including edging

### MATERIALS

**5** LION BRAND Homespun
*6 oz (170 g) 185 yd (169 m) Skein*
*98% Acrylic, 2% Polyester*

- 2 skeins #311 Rococo (A)
- 3 skeins #318 Sierra (B)
- 2 skeins #347 Mediterranean (C)
- 3 skeins #326 Ranch (D)
- 3 skeins #335 Prairie (E)
- 2 skeins #338 Nouveau (F)
  or colors of your choice
- Sizes L-11 and N-13 (8 and 9 mm) crochet hooks OR SIZE TO OBTAIN GAUGE

### GAUGE

4.5 + 6.5 rows = 4" (10 cm) on larger hook.

BE SURE TO CHECK YOUR GAUGE.

### NOTES

This afghan is worked sideways with the stripes running top to bottom. When changing colors, begin new color in the last loop of double crochet of previous row.

### AFGHAN

With F and larger hook, ch 95.

**Row 1** Draw up a loop in 5th ch from hook, yarn over, draw up another loop in same ch, yarn over, draw up another loop in same ch; skip 1 ch and draw up a loop through next ch—7 loops on hook. Yarn over and draw through all 7 loops; ch 1 (cluster made).
*Draw up a loop in same ch where last loop was drawn, yarn over, draw up another loop through same ch, yarn over, draw up another loop through same ch; skip 1 ch and draw up a loop through next ch—7 loops on hook. Yarn over and draw through all 7 loops; ch 1 (made). Repeat from * across. Dc in last ch (where last loop of last cluster was drawn); turn—45.

**Row 2** Ch 3, begin in ch-1 at end of last of previous row and continue to work all in the ch-1s to end of row; dc in same st (where last loop of last cluster was drawn); turn.
*Change to E and work row 2 times.
Change to D and work row 2 times.
Change to C and work row 2 times.
Change to B and work row 2 times.
Change to A and work row 2 times.
Continue working 2 rows in each color and complete the color sequence as follows: B, C, D, E, F*; rep from * 3 more times (41 total stripes). Fasten off.

**Note** This edging is about 5" (12.5 cm) wide.

**Round 1** With RS facing, A, and smaller hook, beg in any corner, ch 3, work 4 dc in same st, *dc in next st, 5 dc in next st (*shell made*); repeat from * along all sides of afghan, ending dc in last st; join with slip stitch to beg ch-3.

**Round 2** With B, slip stitch in first 2 dc, ch 3, work 4 dc in same st, *skip 2 dc, dc in next dc, skip 2 dc, 5 dc in next dc (3rd dc of shell on previous round); repeat from *, ending skip 2 dc, dc in last dc; join with slip stitch to beg ch-3.

**Rounds 3–5** Repeat round 2 using C, D, and E.

**Round 6** With F, repeat rnd 2, but work 6 dc for each shell. Fasten off. Weave in ends.

# The Lattice Throw

In its first rendition, this beautifully textured knit blanket was made for a baby, using stark white yarn, and trimmed in pink or blue to suit the needs of the nursery. We increased the size and gauge, then chose more grownup colors. The resulting piece is the perfect companion for a chilly day.

KNIT **EASY**

## SIZE
50" x 70" (127 x 178 cm)

## MATERIALS
LION BRAND Homespun

*6 oz (170 g) 185 yd (169 m) Skein*

*98% Acrylic, 2% Polyester*

- 5 skeins #322 Baroque (MC)
- 3 skeins #321 Williamsburg (CC) or colors of your choice
- Size 11 (8 mm) knitting needles OR SIZE TO OBTAIN GAUGE

## GAUGE
11 sts + 20 rows = 4" (10 cm) in Garter Stitch (k every row).

BE SURE TO CHECK YOUR GAUGE.

**NOTE** Carry CC up side of fabric. Use MC to catch it every other row.

## PATTERN STITCH
**(multiple of 8 sts + 6)**

**Note** Slip all sts as if to p. Slip with yarn in back, unless otherwise noted.

**Row 1 (RS)** With CC, knit.

**Row 2** With CC, knit.

**Rows 3, 5, 7, and 9** With MC, k 2, slip 2, *k 6, slip 2; repeat from *, ending k 2.

**Rows 4, 6, 8, and 10** With MC, k 2, *slip 2 with yarn in front, k 6; repeat from *, ending slip 2, k 2.

**Rows 11 and 12** With CC, k.

**Rows 13, 15, 17, and 19** With MC, *k 6, slip 2; repeat from *, ending k 6.

**Rows 14, 16, 18, and 20** With MC, *k 6, slip 2 with yarn in front; repeat from *, ending k 6. Repeat rows 1–20 for pattern.

## BOTTOM BORDER
With CC, cast on 138 sts.

**Row 1 (RS)** Knit.

**Row 2** K2tog, k to last 2 sts, k2tog—136 sts.

**Row 3** Knit.

**Row 4** K2tog, k to last 2 sts, k2tog—134 sts.

## BODY
With MC, work in Pattern Stitch, beg with Row 3. Continue in pattern until piece measures 68" (172.5 cm) or desired length, ending with row 10 or row 20.

## TOP BORDER
**Row 1 (RS)** With CC, knit.

**Row 2** K into front and back of first st, k to last st, knit into front and back of last st—136 sts.

**Row 3** Knit.

**Row 4** K into front and back of first st, k to last st, k into front and back of last st—138 sts. Bind off loosely.

## SIDE BORDERS

With RS facing and CC, pick up and knit 172 sts along side edge.

**Row 1 (WS)** K into front and back of first st, k to last st, k into front and back of last st—174 sts.

**Row 2** Knit.

**Row 3** K into front and back of first st, k to last st, k into front and back of last st—176 sts. Bind off loosely. Repeat for remaining side.

## FINISHING

Sew corners of Border together. Weave in ends.

Block afghan by soaking in warm water for 5 minutes. Spin out water. Lay flat on floor or bed until dry.

# The Romantic Embossed-Leaf Throw

This is another pretty piece that started out as a baby blanket, but we're sure you'll agree that the sculptural stitches and artful edging make it the perfect accent for a sunroom settee or a bedside chair. What began as a small stitch pattern has evolved into large leaves, the result of substituting a bulky yarn for a baby yarn. Vive la différence!

KNIT with CROCHET edging **EASY**

## SIZE
43" x 80" (109 x 203 cm)

## MATERIALS
**(5)** LION BRAND Landscapes
*1³/₄ oz (50 g) 55 yd (50 m) Ball*
*50% Wool, 50% Acrylic*
- 23 balls #271 Rose Garden or color of your choice
- Size 11 (8 mm) knitting needles OR SIZE TO OBTAIN GAUGE
- Size L-11 (8 mm) crochet hook

**Note** For ease in working, use a circular needle at least 24" (60 cm) long.

## GAUGE
9.5 sts + 16 rows = 4" (10 cm) in Pattern Stitch, blocked. (Embossed leaf counts as one stitch.)

BE SURE TO CHECK YOUR GAUGE

## STITCH EXPLANATION
**Sk2p** Slip one, k2tog, pass slipped stitch over the k2tog stitch.

## PATTERN STITCH (multiple of 6 stitches + 5)
**Note** Stitch count varies from row to row, but will revert to original number at the end of rows 5 and 11.

**Row 1** (RS) P 5, *(k 1, yarn over, k 1) in next st, p 5; repeat from *.

**Rows 2 and 4** K 5, *p 3, k 5; repeat from *.

**Row 3** P 5, *k 3, p 5; repeat from *.

**Row 5** P 5, *sk2p, p 5; repeat from *.

**Row 6** K 5, *p 1, k 5; repeat from *.

**Row 7** P 2, *(k 1, yarn over, k 1) in next st, p 5; repeat from *, ending (k 1, yarn over, k 1) in next st, p 2.

**Rows 8 and 10** K 2, *p 3, k 5; repeat from *, ending p 3, k 2.

**Row 9** P 2, *k 3, p 5; repeat from *, ending k 3, p 2.

**Row 11** P 2, *sk2p, p 5; repeat from *, ending sk2p, p 2.

**Row 12** K 2, *p 1, k 5; repeat from *, ending p 1, k 2.

Repeat rows 1–12 for pattern.

## THROW
Using long tail method (see Techniques, page 188), cast on 101 sts. P 1 row. K 1 row. Work in Pattern Stitch until piece measures 78" (198 cm) or desired length, ending with row 6 or row 12. P 1 row. K 1 row. Bind off very loosely.

## EDGING

**Round 1** With crochet hook, work 3 sc for every 4 sts along top and bottom; 2 sc for every 3 rows along sides; and 3 sc in each corner. Join with slip stitch to beg sc.

**Round 2** Ch 1, work reverse sc (see Techniques, page 188) in each sc around, working 3 reverse sc in corner sc. Join with slip stitch to top of beg ch.

Fasten off.

## FINISHING

Weave in ends.

Block afghan by soaking in warm water for 5 minutes. Spin out water.

Lay flat on floor or bed until dry.

# The Picot-Edge Blanket

This snuggly cabled piece was originally intended as a blanket to keep baby cozy. We've updated it with a more sophisticated palette and a chunky yarn that makes for fast knitting. While you can certainly work it up in a thinner yarn for your favorite little one, we think it's just as suitable tossed over the sofa.

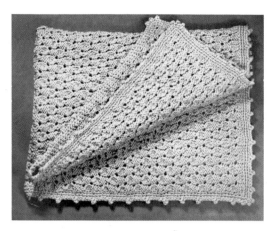

KNIT with CROCHET edging **EASY**

## SIZE
46½" x 68" (118 x 173 cm)

## MATERIALS
 LION BRAND Wool-Ease Chunky
*80% Acrylic, 20% Wool*
*5 oz (140 g) 153 yd (140 m) Ball*
- 11 balls #115 Bay Harbor (MC)
- 1 ball #139 Huckleberry (CC)
  or colors of your choice
- Size 10.5 (6.5 mm) knitting needles
  OR SIZE TO OBTAIN GAUGE
- Size K-10.5 (6.5 mm) crochet hook

**Note** For ease in working, use a circular needle at least 24" (60 cm) long.

## GAUGE
12 sts + 18 rows = 4" (10 cm) in Pattern Stitch, blocked.
BE SURE TO CHECK YOUR GAUGE.

## STITCH EXPLANATION
**Sk2p** Slip one, k2tog, pass slipped stitch over the k2tog stitch.

## PATTERN STITCH
**Note** Work edge sts in St st (k on RS, p on WS).
**Row 1 (RS)** Edge st, *k 3, p 3; repeat from * to last st, 1 edge st.
**Rows 2–3** Edge st, *k 3, p 3; repeat from * to last st, 1 edge st.
**Row 4** Edge st, *yarn over, sk2p, yarn over, p 3; repeat from * to last st, 1 edge st.
**Rows 5–7** Edge st, *p 3, k 3; repeat from * to last st, 1 edge st.
**Row 8** Edge st, *p 3, yarn over, slip 1, k2tog, sk2p, yarn over; repeat from * to last st, 1 edge st.
Repeat rows 1–8 for pattern.

## BLANKET
With MC, cast on 134 sts. Work in Pattern Stitch, beginning with ROW 2. Continue in pattern until piece measures 66" (167.5 cm) from beg, or to desired length, ending with row 2 or row 6. Bind off in pattern.

## EDGING
**Round 1** With crochet hook and MC, work 3 sc for every 4 sts along top and bottom; 2 sc for every 3 rows along sides; and 3 sc in each corner. Join with slip stitch to beg sc.
**Round 2** With CC, sc in each sc around, working 3 sc in corner sc. Join with slip stitch to beg sc.
**Round 3 (Picot edge)** With MC, *3 sc, ch 3, slip stitch in last sc made; repeat from * around, working 3 sc in corner sc. Join with slip stitch to beg sc.
Fasten off.

Weave in ends. Block afghan by soaking in warm water for 5 minutes.
Spin out water. Lay flat on floor or bed until dry.

# The Hot Property

Before the days of electric blankets (and reliable heating), the best way to warm the cold sheets was to tuck a hot water bottle under the covers. These old-fashioned comforts have undergone somewhat of a revival of late, so we offer this reinterpretation of the classic cover, crocheted in bright green with hot-pink accents.

## CROCHET **EASY**

### SIZE

**Circumference** 17 ½" (44.5 cm)
**Length** 14" (35.5 cm)

### MATERIALS

**(5)** LION BRAND Wool-Ease Chunky
*5 oz (140 g) 153 yd (140 m) Ball*
*80% Acrylic, 20% Wool*
- 1 ball # 130 Grass (MC)
- 1 ball # 140 Deep Rose (CC)
  or colors of your choice
- Size K-10.5 (6.5 mm) crochet hook
  OR SIZE TO OBTAIN GAUGE
- Scraps of contrasting yarn to be
  used as markers
- Large-eyed, blunt needle

### GAUGE

10 sts + 11 rows = 4" (10 cm) in Stripe Pattern.
BE SURE TO CHECK YOUR GAUGE.

### PATTERN STITCH

**STRIPE PATTERN (multiple of 4 sts)**
**Round 1** *Sc in back loop of first 2 sts, sc in front loop of next 2 sts; repeat from * around. Repeat round 1 for Stripe Pattern.

### HOT WATER BOTTLE COVER

With MC, ch 28; join with slip stitch to form ring.
**Round 1** Ch 1, sc in each ch around—28 sc. Mark first and 15th stitches and work in a spiral.
**Rounds 2–5** Work 3 sc in first st, sc in each st to marked st, 3 sc in marked st, sc in each st to end of round—44 sc.
Change to Stripe Pattern and work in a spiral until Cover measures 10" (25.5 cm) from beg or desired length. Join with slip stitch to beg sc.
**Next round** Ch 3, dc in next 9 sts, 2 dc in next st, *dc in next 10 sts, 2 dc in next st; repeat from * around; join with slip stitch to top of beg ch-3—48 dc.
**Next round** Ch 3 (dc, ch 3, 2 dc) in first st, skip 2 sts, sc in next st, skip 2 sts, *(2 dc, ch 3, 2 dc) in next st, skip 2 sts, sc in next st, skip 2 sts; repeat from * around; join with slip stitch to top of beg ch-3. Fasten off.

### FINISHING

**Ties** With 2 strands of CC held together, make 2 ch each 12" (30.5 cm) long. Weave in and out though dc round. Make small tassels (see page 114) and attach to ends of Ties.
(Optional) Beg at bottom of Cover, weave CC under front loop of each sc in rounds 1–5.
Sew bottom seam for 1" (2.5 cm) on either side of center, leaving hole for bottle.
Weave in ends.

# Techniques

### 3 Needle Bind Off

Hold two needles (each with an equal number of stitches) parallel with ends pointing in the same direction. **1.** Using 3rd needle, knit 2 sts together (one st from front needle and one st from back needle), **2.** *knit 2 sts together (one st from front needle and one st from back needle, there are now 2 sts on right hand needle), **3.** pass first st worked over 2nd to bind off; repeat from * across to last st. Cut working yarn and pull through last st to secure. ▼

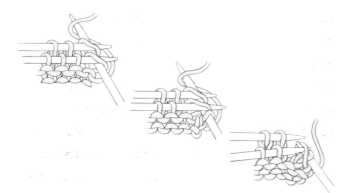

### SSK (slip, slip, knit)

**1.** Slip next 2 sts as if to knit, one at a time, to right-hand needle; **2.** insert left-hand needle into fronts of these 2 sts and k them tog.

### SSP (slip, slip, purl)

**1.** Slip next 2 sts as if to knit, one at a time, to right needle; pass them back to left-hand needle; purl them together through back loops. ▼

### FPDC (front post double crochet)

Yarn over, insert hook from front to back then to front, going around the dc post, draw up a loop, (yarn over and draw through 2 loops on hook) twice. Skip st behind the FPDC.

### M1 (make 1)

An increase worked by placing the tip of left hand needle (either from front to back or back to front (see following) under the horizontal thread lying between needles and placing it onto left-hand needle. This loop can either be knit or purled.

### M1R (make one, leaning right)

**1.** Bring the tip of left-hand needle from back to front under the horizontal thread lying between the needles and place loop on needle. **2a & b.** Knit (or purl) this loop. One right-leaning st has been added. ▼

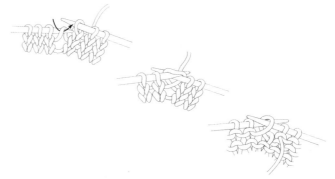

### M1L (make one, leaning left)

**1.** Bring the tip of the left hand needle from front to back under the horizontal thread lying between the needles and place loop on needle. **2a & b.** Knit (or purl) through the back of the loop. One left-leaning st has been added. ▼

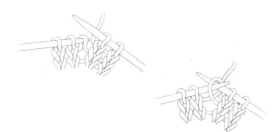

### Double base ch/sc (-Base chain/single crochet)

**1.** Start with a slip knot, chain 2. **2.** Insert hook in 2nd chain from hook, draw up a loop. **3.** Yarn over and draw through 1 loop. **4.** Yarn over and draw through 2 loops—1 single crochet with its own chain at bottom. Work next stitch under loops of that chain. Insert hook under 2 loops of bottom of previous stitch, draw up a loop, yarn over and draw through 1 loop, yarn over and draw through 2 loops. Repeat for length of foundation. ▼

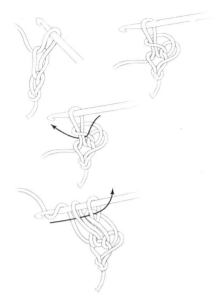

### Reverse SC (also known as Crab or Shrimp stitch)

With the RS of work facing and working *in the opposite direction* that you would normally crochet (i.e., left to right for righthanders; right to left for lefthanders), *insert the hook into the next stitch, yarn over and pull loop through; yarn over again and pull the yarn through the 2 loops on the hook. Repeat from * from rev sc. This makes a decorative, corded edging. ▼

### Cable Cast On

Make a slip knot and put on left-hand needle. Put right-hand needle into slip knot knitwise, wrap yarn around the needle as if to knit and pull loop through. *Leave loop on left-hand needle. Put right-hand needle *between* the two loops on the left-hand needle, wrap yarn around the needle and pull loop through. Repeat from * until total number of stitches are cast on.

### Provisional Cast On

Using a smooth waste yarn and a crochet hook larger than the knitting needles you are using for your project, crochet a chain for at *least* as many cast on sts as indicated in pattern. Fasten off and tie a knot in the end of the yarn (this is the end from which you will "unzip" the chain). 1) Using project yarn and knitting needle, pick up one stitch in each back bump along the crochet chain (one per every cast on st indicated). When indicated in pattern, "unzip" crochet chain and put open loops on knitting needle. Work as specified. ▼

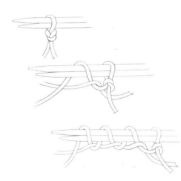

### Long Tail Cast On

Leaving a long tail (at least 3 times longer than the edge that you are casting on), place a slip knot on the needle. Hold the needle in your right hand and the two ends of the yarn in your left fist. Coming down from above the two ends, insert your left index finger and thumb between the two ends to separate them. The yarn from the ball should be over your index finger; the tail should be over your thumb. Hold your fingers upwards as shown. **1.** Bring the needle under the loop on your thumb, then go over-and-under the loop on your index finger. **2.** Slip the loop on your thumb over the loop on the needle and let go. **3.** Gently tighten. Repeat from 1 until you have cast on the number of stitches needed. ▼

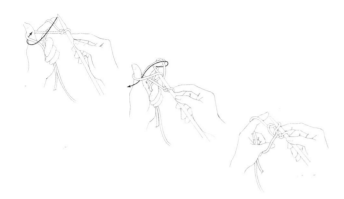

## Invisible Seam (also known as mattress st or woven seam)

Used on side-seams. Lay sections right side up with corresponding stitches aligned. Insert blunt needle under horizontal thread between first and second stitch on the left section, pull yarn through; then insert needle under horizontal thread between first and second stitch on right section and pull through. Continue going back and forth between corresponding horizontal threads until top of seam is reached. Do not pull the seaming thread too tight— the seam should remain as stretchable as the rest of the knitting. ▼

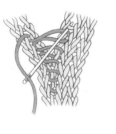

## I-Cord

Using Long-tail method, cast on number of stitches indicated (usually between 2-5). * Do not turn. Pass stitches from left hand needle back to right hand needle so that RS is facing and yarn is coming from the left rear of the stitches. Knit all stitches. Repeat from * until cord is desired length. Periodically pull on cord to even up the stitches.

## I-Cord Bind Off

With WS of fabric to be bound off facing and using simple back loop method, cast on number of stitches desired in cord (for this example we will do a 3-stitch I-cord). *K2, ssk (you are joining i-cord cast on sts to open loops on needle). Pass 3 sts back to right hand needle. Repeat from * to end. Fasten off last 3 sts. This is a firm, non-stretchy bind-off.

# Selected Bibliography

Carroll, Alice. *Complete Guide to Modern Knitting and Crocheting.* New York: Wm. H. Wise & Co., 1942.

Fryer, Jane Eayre. *The Mary Frances Knitting and Crocheting Book.* Berkeley, California: Lacis Publications, 1997. Originally published in 1918 by the John C. Winston Co., Philadelphia.

*Knitting: 19th Century Sources.* Berekley, CA: Lacis Publications, 1998.

*Lion Yarn Book.* New York: The Lion Yarn Co., 1916.

Macdonald, Anne L. *No Idle Hands: The Social History of American Knitting.* New York: Ballantine Books and Toronto: Random House of Canada Ltd., 1988.

*Mil Anys de Disseny en Punt.* Terrassa, Espana: Centre de Documentacio i Museu Textil, 1997.

Newton, Deborah. *Designing Knitwear.* Newtown, CT: Taunton Press, 1992.

*Piecework Magazine Presents a Facsimile Edition of Weldon's Practical Needlework.* 12 vols et seq. Loveland, CO: Interweave Press, 1999–2005.

Paludan, Lis. *Crochet: History and Technique.* Loveland, Colorado: Interweave Press, 1995.

Rutt, Richard. *A History of Hand Knitting.* Loveland, Colorado: Interweave Press, 1987.

Scott, Shirley A. *Canada Knits.* Scarborough, Ontario: McGraw-Hill Ryerson Ltd., 1990.

Sundbo, Annemor. *Everyday Knitting—Treasures from a Ragpile.* Norway: Torridal Tweed, 2000.

Thomas, Mary. *Mary Thomas's Knitting Book.* New York: Dover Publications, 1972. Originally published in 1938 by Hodder and Stoughten, Ltd., London.

—— *Mary Thomas's Book of Knitting Patterns.* New York: Dover Publications, 1972. Originally published in 1943 by Hodder and Stoughton, Ltd., London.

Waller, Jane. *Classic Knitting Patterns from the British Isles: Men's Hand-knits from the 20's to the 50's.* London: Thames and Hudson Ltd., 1984.

# Index